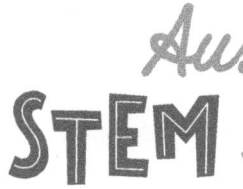

GISELA KAPLAN

Bird and primate scientist

Aussie
STEM Stars

GISELA KAPLAN

Bird and primate scientist

Story told by EMILY GALE

WILD
DINGO
PRESS

Aussie STEM Stars series
Published by Wild Dingo Press
Melbourne, Australia
books@wilddingopress.com.au
wilddingopress.com.au

This work was first published by Wild Dingo Press 2021
Text copyright © Emily Gale

The moral right of the author has been asserted.

Cover Design: Gisela Beer
Illustrations: Diana Silkina
Series Editor: Catherine Lewis
Printed in Australia

Gale, Emily 1975-, author.
Gisela Kaplan: Bird and primate scientist / Emily Gale

A catalogue record for this
book is available from the
NATIONAL
LIBRARY   National Library of Australia
OF AUSTRALIA

ISBN: 9781925893465 (paperback)
ISBN: 9781925893472 (epdf)
ISBN: 9781925893489 (epub)

Every living thing on this planet has a right to be,
has intrinsic value and deserves empathy
and due regard for its needs.
— **Gisela Kaplan**

Contents

1

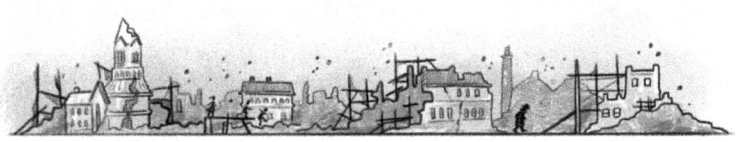

Waiting for Nan

Inside a small unit in Berlin, everything was quiet and still. *Almost* everything. That morning Gisela was like a city sparrow: alert and restless. It was Nan's day. The best day. She felt lighter than she had all week at school, as if her bones were hollow on Sundays.

Gisela climbed from the wooden cot without a sound because it was important not to wake her parents. The cot had been her bed for seven years, but it was that or the floor and she knew better than to complain. Her mother's temper was unpredictable. Though small for her age, by now

Gisela's legs hung out between the bars so it was a relief to get up and stretch. She stood by the window watching a clear dawn. It was spring, she could tell by the blackbirds' song, which meant no shivering as she got dressed and no ice crystals on the inside of the glass. Berlin winters were cruel when you were poor.

A door slammed in the next-door unit and startled her. She pressed her ear to the wall of the room where her parents slept. Luckily, nothing stirred. Her father worked long hours in the day and studied at night. He was one of the lucky ones to have secured an apprenticeship after the war, but they were living on the edge with his meagre pay.

*

The worst war in history had ended six years ago and the scars were deep. There were scars Gisela could see every day, like rubble in the streets, or a church with a bombed spire; a neighbour whose leg finished at his knee, or a stranger collapsed in the street from hunger. And there were scars she couldn't see but sensed in the people she lived among. A terrible sadness that wouldn't go away.

Gisela already knew that people could be broken on the inside.

Her clothes were handmade by her mother, using any scrap of material she could find. Her stripy jumper was only patterned that way because it had been knitted using hundreds of different lengths of wool. This was one of the reasons why school was miserable. There was no uniform and almost every other girl was from a wealthy family, so Gisela's clothes drew the wrong kind of attention.

She was small and wiry with dark hair while her schoolmates were mostly blonde with the bluest eyes. The Nazis under Hitler's rule had wanted a whole race of blonde and blue-eyed people to populate Germany. Millions of people who didn't fit their description of an ideal human had been sent to concentration camps*. There they had been starved, beaten, used for medical experiments and sent to the gas chambers.

Germany wasn't ruled by Nazis anymore but Gisela was still treated by some as a misfit. Just the sight of her turned girls at school sour. They thought she didn't belong. Gisela didn't really understand why she was there either, only that her father had pleaded with the authorities to give her a place. The school had a reputation for expecting hard work and the highest results. To her father it was some compensation for what families like theirs had lost when the Nazis were in power.

Gisela's grandfather came from Eastern Europe and, with that background, such families were declared stateless under Hitler even though Gisela's parents were born in Berlin.

She crept to the kitchen where there was a gas stove, a small sink, a single chair and barely room for two people to stand. All she'd eaten yesterday was a hunk of rye bread dipped in watery barley soup. Every day she hoped for at least as much as she'd eaten the day before. Any less and Gisela thought she'd end up like the bodies in the street that didn't move. If people weren't dying of starvation, they were dying of pneumonia or typhoid fever. Gisela had seen people stumbling in the street and going down with a thump. She was warned to stay away from them because they could be infectious.

> After the war, from 1945 to 1949, millions of people in Germany died from hunger.

She found a small piece of bread which she ate hastily, leaving enough for her parents. Half a loaf had to last the three of them a week. Mostly their food came from a can or was made of powder – powdered milk, powdered soup, powdered egg. Their only vegetables were potatoes, cabbage and onions. Gisela had never tasted meat. Sometimes she was so hungry that she ate nettles.

She checked the time. Nan had promised to come as early as possible but it was a long way by train. Getting up at dawn had been optimistic, even when it came to magical Nan.

During the food shortages in West Berlin after the war, the Allies sent in large quantities of powdered food because it was easier to transport and distribute.

Gisela's grandmother was so special that when she walked into a room, people seemed to fall under her spell. They'd stop what they were doing. Not because Nan was tall or grand or loud; she was none of those things. It was hard to explain but Nan had a kind of light inside her.

After she'd tidied up any evidence that she'd been in the kitchen, she returned to the other room.

A good use of her time would be to practise her words like Nan had suggested. Gisela's stutter meant that her words didn't always come out as she planned. Words would get stuck at the beginning or halfway through. And the harder she tried to force the word out of her mouth, the more frustrating it was. Just one more thing that made her an outcast at school, besides her homemade clothes and where she lived. The girls teased her every time she spoke, which made her stutter even more.

Gisela had told Nan the truth about the bullying on their last outing together – a walk through the towering trees of the nearby forest.

'I hate my stutter, Nan,' she'd confessed. 'It gives me all this trouble. But what can I do?'

The sunlight was playing hide-and-seek in the branches. Gisela felt the strangeness of looking at something beautiful while feeling such pain. Nan had taken Gisela's hands into hers and given her granddaughter a reassuring smile.

'It's *your* stutter, *you* can change it,' Nan had told her. 'This week we will start a secret project. Stand at the mirror each day. Say the sounds and words that give you trouble out loud and watch your lips carefully. Can you do that, Gisela?'

'Yes, I can do that. Will it work?'

'If you have hope and determination, that is all you need.'

Gisela saw the light in Nan's face. In that moment she was thinking of everything she knew about her grandmother. Nan had survived a labour camp run by Nazis. She was one of millions forced to produce supplies for the German war effort. The life Nan had endured there was brutal. There was little food and no comfort. Nan had used straw to brush her teeth and the camps were rife with disease. Yet her spirit was unbroken. Nan was neither bitter nor defeated. She still smiled and she had so much love to give to her granddaughter. Gisela wanted to be like Nan and not let *her* spirit be broken. Since that day in the forest, she'd been practising in the mirror.

From 1933-1945, over 20 million people were forced to work in Nazi labour camps. Conditions were so bad that many did not survive.

She stood in front of it now. While the blackbirds sang outside, she tried a sentence she'd picked out for herself.

'L-L-L-...' She stopped and took a breath. 'L-L-L-...' She stopped again.

'*Lass.*' Gisela smiled at her reflection. It was the quickest she'd ever said that word since the start of the secret project. *Lass* meant *leave*. The rest was *mich allein*. *Lass mich allein*. Leave me alone. It was what she'd like to say to the bullies at school.

For now, she kept on trying, waiting for Nan to come.

2

Berlin Zoo

Gisela hadn't been to a zoo before. Holding Nan's hand as they boarded the train, she couldn't decide whether to be excited or afraid. How close would she get to the animals? Could wild animals be trusted? There were stray dogs all over the city and many of them had rabies*. A few years ago a German Shepherd had come charging at Gisela and knocked her down in the street. Passers-by had screamed as she looked up into a large mouth brimming with sharp teeth. Although the dog had left her alone after that, she'd hit her head badly and the moment had stayed with her. She'd never told anyone.

Passing at speed through the underground tunnels, Nan talked about what had happened to the animals of Berlin Zoo in the war.

World War II was a complicated global war with two main sides. On one side – the Axis – Germany, Italy and Japan. On the other side – the Allies, including Britain, France, the Soviet Union and the USA, and countries that signed the Declaration of the United Nations (including Australia, New Zealand, China, India and Canada).

Early on in the war, the German army had invaded several countries in Europe as well as the Soviet Union, and bombed London and other British cities for many months. Later, Britain and its allies retaliated by bombing German cities. For the next two years there were frequent attacks on Berlin. The zoo became part of the battlefield.

Some of the animals were evacuated to other parts of Germany – just like children all over Europe had been evacuated to get them out of the way of the fighting. But most were left behind to be killed in explosions or

Before the war, there had been 3,500 animals in the zoo. By the end, there were only 91.

fires. Animals that survived the bombs often died afterwards of shock.

By 1944, the tide had turned and Germany was on the losing side of the war. Then, in April 1945, came the Battle of Berlin when the Soviet army bombed the city in a final push for victory. The battle was so fierce that most of the city was destroyed and there was nowhere for the remaining zoo animals to hide. Giraffes, elephants, antelopes, crocodiles . . . they were all in the firing line and most of them perished.

'Why didn't we keep all the animals safe, Nan?' Gisela asked. 'It wasn't their fault there was a war.'

'There weren't enough people who wanted to help animals instead of just themselves,' said Nan. 'People were afraid for their lives. They weren't thinking about the animals then.'

'Did any of them escape the zoo?'

'Some did but they were recaptured. There was a dingo, I remember – do you know what a dingo is?' Gisela shook her head. 'It's a wild dog from Australia.'

Gisela intended to avoid wild dogs. But she knew Australia was as far away as you could get;

she wondered how the dingo had got to Berlin and whether it had been sad to leave its home.

'Of course, many birds would have escaped,' Nan went on. 'Wings are useful like that.'

Gisela gave her grandmother a small smile but she was still thinking about all the innocent animals caught up in the war.

'Let me tell you about the animals they *could* save,' suggested Nan.

Gisela liked the story of Knautschke, the hippo, born in 1943. Knautschke's mum had been killed when bombers destroyed the hippo house. Brave animal keepers poured water over Knautschke to keep him alive, and many Berliners brought food for him even though they barely had enough for themselves. Nan said that Knautschke had survived because of this kindness; he would be one of the animals Gisela would see that day.

> An alligator called Saturn, who survived the war in the Berlin Zoo and was later moved to Moscow Zoo, lived until 2020!

All the same, after hearing Nan's stories, in Gisela's head the zoo was covered in rubble and poor dead animals, with confused survivors walking among them. She was relieved as soon as she saw the grand gates and the smiling visitors. The war was in the past. Of course, Nan would never take her somewhere frightening.

Sticking close to her grandmother, Gisela walked and talked for hours. There was Knautschke the hippo, as well as other animals that had survived the war: lions, hyenas and chimpanzees. She liked the Hamadryas baboons with their silver manes and pink faces. And a beautiful black stork, nearly as tall as her, with red legs and a beak to match.

'So, what do you think of the zoo?' asked Nan.

There was a lot Gisela wanted to say but none of it was ready to come out. She was rolling all the new names she'd learnt around in her head. That was alright with Nan. There was no rush and no need to worry when she was with her grandmother. It was completely different from every other day of the week.

They were heading back to Knautschke's enclosure for feeding time when something caught Gisela's eye. A furry creature lay next to the path. It was very still, chained to a post, and covered in the dust being kicked up by people's shoes.

Gisela went to it and knelt down. It was a small grey fox.

'Nan, can I touch it?' she asked. Her grandmother nodded. Gently, Gisela put her hand on its fur. It didn't flinch or snarl but seemed to like it. Gisela was struck by a feeling of sadness; she found it hard to breathe. This little grey fox was abandoned, powerless. No one else had even noticed it. What kind of a life did it have?

'I can't leave the fox here, Nan. Can we save it? Can we take it home with us?'

Nan bent down and put her hand on Gisela's back. 'We can't do that, but we will see what else we can do.'

They found a tin bowl and a tap and brought the little fox a drink, for which it seemed grateful. As it lapped the water, Gisela brushed the dust from its skinny body. Then she carried it from the hot concrete to a patch of grass.

Gisela looked at the fox and the fox looked back at her. If only she could take off those heavy chains.

Nan promised that she would speak to the management of the zoo about their treatment of this animal. But as they continued to walk around, Gisela saw things differently: the bleak concrete of the bear pit, the small pool of water for a giant elephant seal, and that heavy chain around the little fox.

3

Someone to care for

It was the middle of summer, 1953; Gisela was nine years old. She sat with her friend Kurt under her favourite archway. The community they lived in was made up of several small streets connected by narrow roads. Each street had neat rows of units, two storeys' high, with small windows and balconies. There were strict rules in place for residents: no noise, no children out after dark, and regular inspections.

Kurt lived with his mother and eight brothers and sisters in a unit just as small as the one Gisela lived in. They often sat here to watch the world go by and to talk about whatever came into their heads.

Gisela was watching Kurt write his name on the wall with a piece of flint.

'You'll get into trouble for that,' she said.

'I won't! We live on the safe side of Berlin,' he answered.

Gisela knew what Kurt meant but she wasn't sure he was right, exactly.

Germany had been split into zones when the war ended and the countries that had defeated Germany had taken one zone each. To make things more complicated, Berlin – the capital city – was also split. West Berlin was governed by the US, Britain and France, each of which had a zone. The American zone was where Gisela and Kurt lived. Meanwhile, East Berlin was governed by the Soviet Union, whose government had very different ideas and rules that people had to follow, with much less freedom. Gisela's other grandmother lived there. She took long train rides to visit Gisela, hiding home-grown vegetables inside her clothing so she wouldn't get robbed for them.

There was even more poverty in East Berlin and jobs were scarce. As Gisela and Kurt were always hungry, it was sometimes hard to believe that there were people who had it even worse. The Communist Party in East Berlin was very strict. They even controlled the kind of music people were allowed to listen to.

'I heard there's another war coming,' said Kurt.

'That can't be true,' Gisela replied with force, more because she hoped it wasn't true than because she knew it wasn't.

Kurt threw the flint over to Gisela and explained.

'Alright, not a war but a big protest over the other side of the city. My mum has a cousin in East Berlin. The workers there are sick of being treated like slaves. There's going to be an uprising against the government.'

Gisela looked out at the quiet streets of their suburb of Zehlendorf. Perhaps to most people there was nothing special about this archway, but to Gisela it separated her two worlds.

On one side there were beautiful forests and cobbled roads. The spacious, leafy estates of the wealthy had rarely been bombed during the war.

That was where Gisela's school was, where she loved her classes but was bullied every day because she came from the poor community.

On the other side was the ghetto of war leftovers that Gisela and Kurt were part of. Cramped units filled with the damaged and the hungry. Bombings had caused a serious lack of housing, and the Berlin Senate kept this part of Zehlendorf for those who'd suffered most under the Nazis during the war.

Gisela's attention was drawn to a line of ants marching like factory workers into a narrow crack in the archway. The ants brought a flash of memory: Gisela and her parents used to live somewhere different – a sweet house that she'd loved, with a tiny garden to play in. They'd had good neighbours: a cellist who'd play Gisela's requests, and a lady who kept a goat in the cellar to protect it from those who might kill it for food. One day, when Gisela was four, she'd been transfixed watching the ants in her garden and she'd picked one up. Not realising how delicate it was, between her little fingers, the ant had stopped wriggling for good.

Not long afterwards, Nan had come to visit and brought with her a new storybook: *The Adventure of Two Ants*. Gisela read the story and studied the pictures closely. When she'd finished, her skin crawled with terrible guilt over the ant she'd killed in order to study its body, as if she had owned its life just because she was bigger and stronger.

As Kurt continued to tell her about the protests in East Berlin, Gisela kept watching the ants, thinking about the way the book was still with her, reminding her to never cause harm to any living thing.

That same evening, Gisela lingered in the doorway while her parents listened to the radio. Kurt was right. Fighting in East Berlin had begun. Thousands of workers had shown up to protest. Soviet flags were burning in the streets. The police had tried to control the uprising and when that failed the Soviet army sent in tanks and soldiers to break them up.

Nearly a million East Germans marched in protest against working conditions and terrible living standards in June 1953. Soviet forces killed over 100 of these demonstrators.

When Gisela's mother turned around and saw her there, she switched off the news, brushed past Gisela and slammed the door. Soon came the sound of the typewriter. Her mother was working as a journalist for a news agency.

'Leave her be, Gisela,' said her father. Gisela didn't need to be warned. She was afraid of her mother, with good reason. Surviving at home meant staying out of the way and being careful with her words. Most days that still wasn't enough to avoid her mother's temper.

Even though the riots were on the Soviet side of Berlin, that didn't seem far enough away to stop thinking about them. Besides, that was where her other grandmother lived; maybe that was the reason her mother had left the room so suddenly. Even with the radio off, Gisela imagined she could still hear the angry chants of the crowds and the sound of bullets.

*

Six months later, it was Christmas. As the hunger crisis in Berlin started to ease, there was a little more food at home. Gisela and her parents had been dangerously malnourished since the war but there was some hope in sight.

On Christmas Eve, the smell of sweet baked apples filled their home. Gisela was reading a book on the rug in the living room, as close to the coal heater as it was safe to be, when her parents came in carrying a large object between them. There was a sheet draped over it.

'Here you are, Gisela,' said her father, smiling.

Under the sheet was a small, blue budgie*. Amazed, Gisela touched the cage with her fingertips.

'For me?' She was not used to presents.

She tried to catch the bird's eye but it would not look at her. It was so quiet, holding onto the bar with its delicate pink claws, a feathered tummy making tiny movements as it breathed. She couldn't believe that her parents had given her something so special. Something that was actually *alive*.

The following day Nan, and Grandma from East Berlin, came to visit. The cage had been put on a small table in the room where Gisela slept. As Nan opened the cage door, Gisela wondered if somehow *she* was behind this surprising gift.

The bird sat so still. It didn't seem to have nibbled the seeds Gisela had put in the metal tray.

'It doesn't like me,' said Gisela.

'No, it's frightened,' Nan told her. 'Give it time. Your job is to make it feel safe.'

Over the next few days, Gisela used every gram of patience. She closed the door of the room so that the bird wouldn't be afraid of her mother's shouting. She put food on the tip of her finger and slowly put her hand inside the cage. And she sang to the bird in a soft voice – tunes she'd learnt at school from operas and folk songs. It bobbed its head as soon as she began.

In only a few weeks, the bird would sit on her finger, fly around her bedroom, land on her shoulder, and even sit close to Gisela's lips as she sang. Nan had believed that Gisela could make the bird feel safe, and she had.

Two years later, Gisela had taught her feathered friend plenty of words. She had named the bird Perle and every day she was grateful for this clever and loving creature.

But then an even more surprising delivery turned up. A baby brother.

4

Stepping stones

From the outside, the Droste-Hülshoff High School was an imposing mansion with a bell tower, turrets, steeply pitched roofs and a carved stone entrance. School hours were Monday to Saturday, eight o'clock until midday. The school's facilities were among the best in Berlin. There were science labs, theatre programmes, orchestras, choirs and excursions. They offered art classes, Latin, Greek, Russian, history, literature, all the sciences, chemistry, algebra and more. But to the wealthy families, Gisela was a cuckoo in the nest, an intruder. Many of them turned up their noses, fearing they'd catch poverty from Gisela's homemade clothes.

Gisela was in her literature class one day, finding it hard to concentrate on the questions about a novel they were reading. Now aged eleven, life at home had become more difficult since her little brother was born. Her mother didn't seem to want him. She wouldn't answer Daniel's cries or prepare his bottle, or change his nappies or rock him to sleep. And since their father worked so much and otherwise kept to himself, when she wasn't at school Gisela was in charge of Daniel.

She was so tired that the words were swimming on the pages of her book.

A well-stocked library was one thing that this school had not yet recovered from the war. The Nazis started book burning years before the war began. From 1933 onwards, books by Jewish authors or anyone considered to be against Nazi politics were destroyed.

Among those books burned by the Nazis were the writings of a German Jewish poet, Heinrich Heine, who wrote in 1821: *Where they burn books, they will also ultimately burn people.*

Gisela felt something sharp on the side of her neck, like an insect bite. The muffled laughter behind her made her realise that she'd been used as target practice again. A moment later, the same sharp pain only this time the object landed on her chair afterwards – a small, sharp pebble from the pathway outside school. Gisela turned to confront the culprit only to find a whole row of children grinning at her in that sickly-sweet way they put on to avoid getting into trouble.

Nan's advice for curing her stutter had worked by now but it seemed there was nothing some children hated more than an outsider.

The girl beside her – Susan – leaned in close to whisper.

'Don't forget the history assignment, Gisela.'

Susan discreetly opened up one of her exercise books to show Gisela what she meant. The assignment was from a class Gisela had missed. Skipping school only got Gisela into more trouble, but she couldn't help it. The truth was she was so desperate some days that she thought about running away. But she couldn't leave Daniel behind so she'd have to take him along with her, and she didn't think they'd survive out there on their own. Susan was the only friend who cared enough to fill Gisela in on what she'd missed.

Nan had told her once, 'There are stones in the river to jump to'. Susan was one of those stones in the river. Nan was another. It was up to Gisela to recognise the *stones in the river* when they came along, because the river was raging.

The bell for the end of school rang at lunchtime and everyone packed up their things to go home. For most of them, a hot meal in a beautiful house awaited them.

The literature teacher, Fräulein Schmidt, called out, 'One moment, Gisela!'

Was she in trouble for daydreaming? Gisela ignored the smug faces of the children filing out of the classroom, who only hoped she'd be in trouble. Susan lingered to give her a friendly smile.

Fräulein Schmidt approached Gisela's desk and crouched down.

'I wanted to tell you about something that I think you'll like very much.'

Gisela's body softened as she realised that she wasn't in trouble after all. She should have known.

Fräulein Schmidt wasn't like the teachers who thought that Gisela didn't belong at the school. She was the daughter of a brave Protestant minister who'd helped Jewish people escape the Nazis.

Although many Germans had shown hatred towards Jewish people and even betrayed their own neighbours to the Gestapo during the war, there were some brave people who'd resisted Hitler's rules. They had risked their lives by hiding Jewish families in their homes or helping them to get false identification papers. They did it knowing that if they were caught, they and their families would be imprisoned or, most likely, killed. Fräulein Schmidt's father had died in a concentration camp.

5,000-7,000 Jewish Berliners went into hiding, but by the end of the war, only about a quarter survived.

The 'something you'll like' that Fräulein Schmidt was telling Gisela about was a mobile library that would be coming to school twice a week. She explained that Gisela would be able to take books home for free, and the selection would be excellent. Books on everything she could think of. Stories to escape into. Facts to fill her head. It was something to look forward to. Another stone in the river.

As Gisela was leaving, Fräulein Schmidt took out an exercise book from the towering pile on her desk.

'One last thing. I wanted to give you back your assignment early. It was excellent.'

Gisela felt her cheeks warm up as she saw the neat, red **A-** on the page. It was almost perfect! The minus had been given for two tiny spelling mistakes.

*

She could hear her baby brother's cries before she reached the unit. Although the afternoon would be tiring – feeding him, changing his nappy, taking him out for some sunshine, putting him to bed – Gisela was still flying high because of the good mark from her teacher, and knew that she could get through it.

Inside, she scooped Daniel out of the cot. It was his now. Gisela had a fold-up bed that she pushed into the corner during the day.

She wiped the tears from his shiny red face and smothered him in kisses.

'Shh, it's alright, I'm here now.'

Her mother was in the other room working on her typewriter. Gisela went in, holding her brother on her hip.

'Look, Mother, from Fräulein Schmidt.' She put the open exercise book down beside her.

Her mother stared at it for a few moments and resumed typing, without a word.

Gisela backed away, feeling foolish and now a little afraid.

'A-*minus*,' her mother said scornfully. And the typewriter keys went *clack-clack-clack*.

*

It looked like an ordinary truck driving down the street. Gisela was in a small crowd of people, standing on tiptoes to get a better look. After the truck parked, two women got out and came around the side to open up a large hatch. Inside were shelves of books and a noticeboard. Gisela had a good feeling about this. It wasn't that she had a list of books she was ready to ask for; it was the thought of being invited to try *any* book. Being poor didn't matter at the mobile library because it was free.

Buses and trams that had been used as mobile libraries before the war were destroyed by the Nazis; people hadn't been free to read whatever they liked under their rule. During the 1950s, in the sector of West Berlin where Gisela lived, the service was introduced again. They were filled with books written in other languages as well as German. Gisela was learning Latin, Greek, French, Italian and Russian at school.

The librarians explained to Gisela that she could take two books on a Tuesday and four books on a Thursday to see her through the weekend. From that day on, Gisela started to read...*everything*. She read about cosmology*, expeditions, and revolutions. She read fact and fiction, poetry and prose, travel and adventure books, classics and lots of science books. Once she'd finished with all the children's books that the library had to offer, they let her choose books from the adult library.

One day the librarian on duty asked her: 'Are you trying to read more books than anyone else?'

Gisela didn't understand what the woman meant. She'd never thought about it like that. She read for herself, not to be in a competition.

She was becoming clever at spotting the stones in the river that Nan had taught her about; this library-on-wheels was another one. She also took the chance to learn judo in free, after-school classes. Smaller and scrawnier than the rich kids, from years of powdered food and daily hunger, Gisela discovered that size didn't matter in the art of self-defence.

Then there was Fräulein Becker, Gisela's art teacher, who paid her special attention just like Fräulein Schmidt, even taking her to art museums. And Gisela was able to take woodwork classes after school on days when her mother was feeling more herself and could look after Daniel, now he was a little older.

But even with all of this, sometimes life at home was miserable and frightening in a way that Gisela couldn't even tell Nan. She dreamed of escaping for good, but a school excursion changed her mind.

As the children walked in twos, they whispered their guesses about where Frau Weber might be taking them. Gisela was privately convinced that it was the zoo since they were heading towards the station, but when Frau Weber took a sharp left Gisela realised she was wrong.

Their teacher stopped outside some tall, iron gates. In the distance, Gisela and Susan could see a large house. Looking closer, they spotted children raking leaves, carrying branches to a huge bonfire, and pushing large wheelbarrows. Gisela thought it looked like a nice day of gardening for the children, until she looked closer.

'What do you see?' asked Frau Weber.

'Just some kids,' shrugged one girl.

'Is this a school?' asked another.

'None of them are smiling,' said Gisela.

'This is a home for orphans and runaways,' Frau Weber explained. 'The children aren't allowed beyond these gates, ever. They spend their days working or taking instruction. The rules in here are very different. Nothing like what you are all used to. If the children don't like the food, they have to eat it anyway. If they vomit because the food makes them ill, they have to eat the vomit.'

'No!' gasped some of the class.

Gisela gripped onto the iron bars of the gates. Worse than the zoo, she thought.

Frau Weber told them more about the lives of the children inside. As Gisela took it in, she tucked away her plans to run away from home. She couldn't take that risk. As Nan had told her, it was important not to just have a Plan A, but a Plan B and C as well.

During the war, many children were orphaned. Afterwards, some were sent to children's homes, and others roamed the forests in search of shelter and food.

*

It was Nan's day and Gisela waited with two-year-old Daniel. As always, they were dressed in homemade clothes, with a home haircut to match, because the family was still short of money. But now she was thirteen, Gisela wondered what it would be like to twirl around the room in a glittery gown of feathers and tulle; to dance at one of Berlin's famous ballrooms, or to have a part in a play or an opera. To be somebody else for an evening was something she let herself dream about sometimes.

Daniel dropped one of her library books on the floor with a *thud* and Gisela came back to reality. While they waited for Nan, she let Daniel help out with Perle, making sure the bird had enough food and water for the day. Although she often let Perle fly around the room where she and Daniel slept, whenever she was out she shut Perle safely inside the cage. It was wise not to let anything upset her mother, though sometimes impossible to avoid. Gisela knew by now that it was her father who had wanted her to have the budgerigar.

Nan took the children to nearby Grunewald forest, where she'd taken Gisela on many of their special days. Gisela didn't mind sharing her grandmother because Nan had never made her feel that she wasn't important, even after Daniel was born. There was enough Nan for both of them.

5

Something to tell you

Thanks to the truckful of books that passed through Zehlendorf twice a week, Gisela's mind could travel far and wide. The scrawny thing who'd been bullied for living in a poor community and wearing homemade clothes was now a top academic student. Whether or not the rich girls at school liked her, they needed her – she was a star of the debating team and competed nationally in athletics. Her favourite activity was long distance running, which made her feel as if she was escaping her troubles for a while. She had to do this in secret because the school believed that marathons were only suitable for boys.

During morning break in the school grounds she often had a group around her to listen to stories she remembered from the books she was reading. Her memory stored them well, turning Gisela into her own kind of mobile library and earning herself a nickname: 'the professor'.

One day she was selected from many others to recite a poem for a visiting writer, Werner Bergengruen, to thank him on behalf of the school for sharing his expertise. The teacher had chosen Bergengruen's poem *Die Meise*, which was about admiring and befriending a tiny bird. Gisela knew all about that because of Perle. And she'd grown to love performing, whether it was dancing, singing, acting or poetry recitals – something she never would have guessed she could do with confidence when she was seven and spoke with a stutter.

When the day arrived, Gisela put her heart into the poem and the audience was captivated. She lingered on the line towards the end:

If only I could understand your voice.

*

It was a Sunday and Gisela was working on a new plan at home while Daniel napped in his cot. At nearly fourteen years old, she wanted to use her position at school to help others. By now she was an expert at travelling between her two different worlds. Attending school in a mansion with every facility she could dream of, her friends had sailing boats and fancy cars and no idea what real hunger felt like. Meanwhile, at home, the children in the units were growing up in severe poverty.

With determination, Gisela had made being an outsider work for her. How could that help others, she wondered? She planned to form a special committee. Their role would be to bring two communities together: young people from non-Jewish and Jewish backgrounds. They would try to heal the terrible damage done by Nazi Germans since the 1930s.

'What are you up to?' her father said.

'Something good, I think,' she replied. 'I want to tell you both about it.'

Gisela's mother stopped her typing and came to listen.

But as Gisela explained her committee, her parents' faces paled. Her father turned his back on her and his body was shaking. Her mother collapsed in a chair and wept.

'What is it? What have I done?' Gisela asked, horrified by their reaction.

At first, they wouldn't answer. But she begged them to tell her. Finally, her mother spoke through tears.

'We didn't want you to know. It seemed for the best after all we'd lost, everything the family had suffered. Gisela, your heritage is Jewish.'

Gisela couldn't speak. She'd never had a clue about this family secret. It held such weight because of what she knew about the Nazis' plan to wipe out all Jewish people in Europe. Her idea to reach out the hand of friendship to the Jewish children in their district suddenly looked very different. *She* was Jewish, or at least had Jewish heritage. The war might have ended but the prejudice in Germany had not. If this got out, her life at school would change.

Suddenly it made sense why they had so few relatives and why her parents would never talk about the past. As her father explained to her then, most of their family from his side had been killed in concentration camps.

As risky as it was, Gisela told her secret to her schoolfriend, Monika. She had to tell *someone* and she'd spent so much time with Monika's family. They'd taken her out on their sailing boat and to ballrooms around Berlin. Monika had shown Gisela kindness by offering her sandwiches at school, which Gisela sometimes accepted because she was so hungry but often refused because she was ashamed that she never had food of her own to share.

But Monika was the wrong choice. She'd been poisoned by anti-Semitism* and spilled Gisela's secret at school. At first there was whispering – *Gisela endears herself to teachers, Gisela manipulates her way to the top, typically Jewish* – but soon the accusations became more open and more vicious until life at school was once again the ordeal it had been when Gisela was young.

Gisela turned to one of her stones in the river, the literature teacher, Fräulein Schmidt.

'Don't worry, leave this to me,' Fräulein Schmidt told her the moment Gisela had explained.

At the start of the next literature class, Fräulein Schmidt sent Gisela on an errand. As she walked up the corridor away from the classroom, she heard a raised voice. It was hard to believe because she'd never heard her beloved teacher shout before, but Fräulein Schmidt was lecturing the class on their treatment of Gisela. Hearing a teacher stand up for her so passionately restored some of her strength.

Gisela realised that *she* had nothing to be ashamed of. In that moment she was making new plans: she would find some Jewish friends, she would learn Hebrew, perhaps join a choir at the synagogue as she loved to sing. She did not *feel*

Jewish but she needed to find out what a Jewish heritage meant to her. And she wasn't going to let other people's prejudice hold her back.

*

Soon after this, Gisela arrived home to find Perle gravely ill. Hunched over at the bottom of the cage, Perle's breathing sounded strange. Although Gisela had noticed changes in her lately – she wasn't eating as much food, she was moulting feathers and she seemed tired more than usual – it was clear now that Perle was very sick.

Taking her gently out of the cage, Gisela held her close to make her feel safe and loved. She didn't want Perle to know how scared and sad she felt in that moment.

The sweet bird, her companion for six years, who'd flown around the room, nibbled her ear and learnt so many words, had fallen ill with a disease that is common to indoor birds. There was no cure.

*

After the loss of Perle, there was another big change for Gisela.

On the night of 12th August 1961, her city became divided in a new way. The East German government put up a wire fence to separate East Berlin from West Berlin. This was to stop East Germans from moving to the west of Germany, where they had more freedom and a democratically elected government. The fence divided families and friendships overnight. Crossing the fence was strictly forbidden, and was punishable by imprisonment or even death.

The wire fence became the concrete **Berlin Wall**: 155 km long, 4 m tall, and heavily guarded day and night. The rest of Germany was also divided by electrified fences between East Germany and West Germany from 1961 to 1989.

By now Gisela had finished school and had not yet decided what to do next, but drastic plans were about to be made for her.

'Pack your things, Gisela, we're leaving as soon as we can,' her mother instructed.

'Leaving the unit? Do we have a new home somewhere else in the city?' she asked.

'Not Berlin. We're going to Munich. It's too dangerous here. Russian tanks are a few kilometres away. There's no way of knowing what will happen here next. We have to leave.'

Gisela did not argue with her parents' decision, but leaving was bittersweet. It was true that there had been years of hunger and misery here, but Gisela still loved the spirit of the city. There were friends she was sad to leave so suddenly, from the Jewish youth group she had joined and from choirs she'd performed with. She also knew that in Berlin a few brave German citizens had helped to hide Jewish families from the Nazis. Now that she understood her heritage, this held an even stronger meaning.

Munich is a large city in the south of Germany, 500 km from Berlin.

6

Sleeping lions

Gisela was getting ready to go out for the night. Like Berlin, Munich was an energetic city. The daydream she'd had years before in the tiny kitchen while she was looking after Daniel was real life now: dancing felt like freedom. She loved getting dressed up. After all, she'd spent her whole childhood in old-fashioned, hand-stitched clothes.

Tonight, Gisela was going to dance at a fancy dress ball until she couldn't feel the ground under her feet. She would never take freedom for granted when, back in Berlin, life on one side of the wall was strictly controlled. Only last week in the papers there was a story about a boy, Peter Fechter, who'd tried to escape over the wall. All Peter had wanted was to choose where to live his life. Soldiers had shot him as he climbed. Onlookers were too afraid of the authorities to help him, so he died right there at the base of the wall. He was eighteen years old, just a year older than Gisela.

Gisela took a taxi to the ballroom. It was dream-like inside, with a dance floor as smooth as water and overhanging chandeliers like glimmering jellyfish.

When the music finally stopped it was well past midnight. Gisela found herself talking to Tomas, who worked at Germany's top circus – Circus Krone – which travelled all around Europe but had its largest venue right there in Munich. She'd seen posters of it on the way to the ballroom that night. The circus had animal acts like polar bears, elephants, tigers, lions, and horses, as well as human acts like clowns, jugglers, acrobats and animal trainers.

'What do you do in the circus?'

'I'm a lion tamer,' he replied. 'Have you ever been close up to a lion?'

'Only about a hundred times,' Gisela joked.

'If you're interested in animals, I can take you right now.' Tomas seemed sincere but surely the idea was ridiculous. She had come out tonight dressed for a ball, not a safari. Then again, she was too curious to say no.

As they walked towards the animal cages, behind the vast main building of the circus, Gisela remembered that particular feeling she'd had at the zoo with Nan years earlier: the discomfort of seeing wild animals in captivity. She didn't think there had been any lions that day at Berlin Zoo. The animal that had made the biggest impression on her was the poor dusty fox.

She took off her sparkling cape thinking it might be confusing for the animals – what creature would they think she was in all those sequins? – and followed Tomas.

'We can meet them properly inside the cage if you're not too scared,' he said.

Gisela couldn't explain why, but she wasn't afraid at all, so she nodded and he turned the key in the lock. They entered the cage and sat barely a metre away from three resting lions.

The magnificent beasts didn't stir. She was struck by their size and beauty. It was such a privilege to be this close to a wild animal, to know that they didn't fear her.

'I have never seen them so calm with a stranger,' said Tomas in disbelief. 'Gisela, this is really rare, please believe me. You could be a lion tamer. I could train you.'

In the 1960s there were so many jobs that women were told they could not do, but strangely enough that did not apply to training wild animals in a circus. As far back as 1908, a woman named Ida Krone had a circus act with fourteen lions.

'Will you consider it?' he continued. 'Look at them, they're like kittens around you. That doesn't happen with just anyone. There's something about you that makes them feel at ease.'

Gisela loved being near them, that much was true. But zoos and circuses were not for her. To make animals perform? And to convince herself that the animal didn't mind, or that they enjoyed it? No matter how popular the Circus Krone was in Germany, it didn't feel right to her.

*

Gisela had lots of dreams about what she could be, but how would she turn the dreams into plans? At this point it seemed as if she could be... *anything!*... She needed to take a leap.

The next morning, a letter arrived telling her that she'd won a scholarship to the Munich Conservatorium to train as an opera singer.

'You are a contralto,' she was told when she started at the Conservatorium. 'This is most fortunate. It is a rare voice, so you will be in demand.'

Contralto is the lowest type of female voice. There was a deep, warm colour to the notes when Gisela sang. And because she was so lucky to have that vocal range, Gisela was offered plenty of singing parts. She started out singing at festivals but that was only the beginning. Opera singing is greatly admired in Europe, and in the 1960s opera was flourishing. Gisela's apprenticeship took her all over Europe.

She sang in Paris at the famous university, the Sorbonne. She sang in Rome to the Pope. She sang at Oxford University in England, and in Ireland at the Cork Music Festival.

> Gisela trained under Elizabeth Hallstein, who had also trained her own daughter, the famous soprano Ingeborg Hallstein.

Gisela could sing operas in German, Italian and French. Each opera told a story and she loved being part of every one of them. After so many performances, she felt confident when she stepped on stage. The only trouble was her sense of humour – sometimes, during a serious part of the opera, like a death scene, Gisela couldn't help but wink at the audience.

But her success didn't change the tensions at home. As difficult as it was to part with her brother, now that she was old enough to leave, she did.

*

'A ticket to Frankfurt, please,' she said at the train station. 'One way.'

Four hours later she arrived, alone, in a brand-new place. Gisela planned to find a job and continue to train as an opera singer.

Frankfurt is in western Germany, on the Main River. Before the war, it was famous for its mediaeval buildings and its warren of narrow streets. The buildings had sat closely together, made of brick and timber, with turrets and beautifully shaped windows, intricate stonework, pointed roofs and pretty chimneys. But like most cities in Germany, bombing had left it in rubble. In the heart of the old town, only one building had survived without damage.

Gisela, who had never known Frankfurt to be any different, loved what she saw that morning. The wide streets were teeming with life: bold new buildings, parks, trees, the river, art galleries, shops and theatres – and there were glimpses of the old

Frankfurt if you looked hard enough. It had all the bright lights of Berlin and Munich but it was a fresh start.

She could be anyone here.

*

In the late 1960s, by the age of 24, Gisela had been married for a while and had a baby daughter. But when the marriage ended, she came up with her bravest plan yet. This time, it would not be a train that would take Gisela and her daughter to the next adventure. It was to be a much longer journey.

7

Long-distance migration

Gisela's plan for a fresh start pointed to Australia. The Australian government had encouraged Europeans to join its population since 1945, with posters and slogans, promises of year-round sunshine and employment. *Big opportunities with space to live! Build your children's future!*

While her daughter, Peta, played next to her, Gisela chatted to a friend about her plan.

'I wonder if we'll be welcome there,' she said. Although it was 1968, during both world wars the Australian government had imprisoned people of

German heritage, including some women and children. Back then, Germans (and Italians and Japanese) were seen as enemies of Australia. This was true even for German-Australian families who'd lived in Australia for generations, people who had never even been to Germany.

Even though Gisela didn't think of herself as German, she spoke the language and had lived there all her life. She was worried that they'd face discrimination.

The other worry was money. A form she'd had to sign committed them to stay in Australia for two years. During that time, Gisela and Peta would not be entitled to any help from the government, even if things were desperate.

Most of all, she hated the idea of being kept in a migrant camp against her will when they arrived. Migrant camps were the places you were taken to as soon as you landed from a foreign country. Although there were schemes to help Europeans to migrate to Australia, Gisela had heard stories that worried her. A few years earlier, Italians and Germans had started a riot in a migrant camp where they'd been held for several months. They were frustrated because they hadn't been able to find jobs and felt as if they were stuck in the camp with no hope of starting the new life that they'd come for.

As it turned out, her friend knew someone in Melbourne who could arrange a job for Gisela before she left Germany. With the name and address of the employer on the forms, the authorities would allow Gisela to avoid the migrant camp.

It sounded promising. She would be working in a large restaurant in the outer suburbs. That meant she could support herself and her daughter with her wages while she figured out how to become part of an opera company in Melbourne. In 1968 there was no easy way to find out this kind of information. Life in Australia looked sunny and spacious, but that was all she knew. It was a huge risk.

There was one more thing Gisela was worried about. 'What about the fact that I can hardly speak a word of English?'

Her friend laughed. 'You already speak four languages, I'm sure you'll learn!'

*

On departure day, Gisela carried two-year-old Peta up the aircraft staircase. She was determined to hide her nerves from her little girl. It wasn't leaving Germany that made her anxious but taking Peta to a foreign country. Despite the long and uncomfortable flight ahead of them, Gisela was wearing a beautiful suit with high heels. She hoped that if she looked smart and respectable, Australians would treat them well.

Once they found their seats, Gisela noticed that many of the other passengers were speaking a language she recognised. They were from a large country in southern Europe that was known then as Yugoslavia. Based on their clothing, Gisela guessed that they were escaping a life of poverty in the countryside as it was very difficult to find work in Yugoslavia. Gisela smiled at them, one migrant to another. No matter what reasons they had for leaving their home countries, or what language they spoke, they had this bold new adventure in common.

Once they were at high altitude, Peta fell asleep and Gisela tried to relax. A couple sitting in the row in front had five children who were all different levels of fidgety. After the first meal was served and Gisela had eaten what she could of the strange food on a plastic tray, she closed her eyes for a moment.

But it wasn't long before her attention was drawn by voices and movement behind her. Peering down the aisle, she noticed that one family was trying to light a small fire in the walkway using newspaper and paper cups!

Jumping out of her seat, Gisela quickly found an air hostess and managed to explain with actions and the few English words she knew that the family over there had forgotten that fire and plane fuel are a dangerous mix!

The rest of the flight was much calmer. Peta slept, woke, ate some food and slept again. Gisela had hours to think about what the next few weeks would be like: how it would feel to be surrounded by people talking in a language she didn't understand, what traditions Australians might have, what fascinating animals and landscapes they would see. She didn't like to think too far into the future. One step at a time. She would have to adapt and there would be much to learn, but hard work had never scared her.

The plane was due to land in Sydney first. Then they'd transfer to another plane headed for Melbourne.

'Wake up,' whispered Gisela. 'Look, we're nearly there.'

The plane tilted over the ocean as they approached Sydney. The sun was rising, casting bold orange hues in the sky. It was a kind of light she'd never seen before. There was the famous harbour bridge she'd seen pictures of, a sprawling city and the huge sails of an opera house that was under construction. Gisela felt something extraordinary: joy, relief, and something unexpected and magical. She thought: *this feels like home.*

*

The cottage was timber with a corrugated iron roof and a brick chimney. It was small and simple but all that mattered was that it was their first home in Melbourne. They'd moved in a few days ago.

Gisela sat in the front room thinking deeply about that wise thing Nan once told her: don't rely on Plan A, make sure you have a Plan B and C just in case.

Last week she'd had to quit her kitchen job. So that was Plan A gone.

Plan B was also a disaster and this was harder to bear. Gisela wanted to take to the stage in Australia just as she had back home when she'd toured Europe as a singer. But last night she'd had tickets to see an opera and there was hardly anyone in the audience. The performance was so dismal that Gisela had decided then and there that her singing career would have to be put on hold. Opera singing was not yet established enough in Australia to guarantee a regular income and Gisela had a child to support. She needed another idea.

Plan C. She could go back to school.

Although Gisela had achieved excellent grades in Germany, those qualifications meant nothing in Australia. She would have to sit exams again to get into university and that meant three things. One, she needed a job that could fit in around her studies. Two, she would have to go to night school*. And three: she must learn English as quickly as possible.

Melbourne was getting warmer and it wasn't even the height of summer yet. There was a bush in one corner of her backyard where a tiny black-and-white bird was fanning out its tail and cheeping.

It was a thrill to see so many birds here. Gisela imagined that she'd never learn all their names.

Everything was new to her. Trees, butterflies, birds, mammals. Food, music, the weather. The way people said hello, what was polite, what was rude, and most of all, being seen as an outsider when Australia already felt like home.

A much larger black-and-white bird appeared on the roof. And a second one in a nearby gum tree. A third one. A fourth! The one on the roof started to sing and the others joined in. The sound was melodious and complex, and fascinating to tune into.

At four o'clock, Gisela switched on the television to find something for her daughter to watch. A cartoon was just beginning – a boy in a red diving suit swimming with a dolphin. Gisela sat on the floor and called to Peta. The cartoon was called *Marine Boy* and it looked interesting. Gisela tried to make out the words in the introduction song...

He is a boy, a very special boy,
powered by propeller shoes, flying sub ahoy!
Whooshing through the water on a friendly
dolphin's back,
racing to the rescue of victims of attack.

As the song ended and the talking began, she noticed that the English was easier to follow than other programmes she'd tried to watch. She could make out a few words here and there. The dolphin was called Splasher and there was a mermaid with green hair called Neptina. It was a Japanese anime dubbed with English voices. Most of the action seemed to happen underwater in a beautiful landscape of seaweeds.

Twenty minutes later, the cartoon ended. Gisela turned around and realised that Peta hadn't watched any of it – she was behind the chair playing contentedly with toy bricks. But it had given Gisela an idea: *this* is how she might learn English. A children's television show with clear dialogue for her to follow. She'd be able to match the words to the actions and objects and slowly work things out.

Feeling a rush of determination, the following morning Gisela went to get the forms to enrol in night school.

*

Gisela needed to be able to pay the rent while she studied. That day, she walked the streets from factory to factory to ask for a job. As she walked it suddenly began to pour with rain, which took her by surprise. She had given away her umbrella before they left Germany because the advertisement for Australian immigration had promised sunshine 365 days of the year!

Every factory turned her away. Gisela wasn't sure if they really had no vacancies or if it was because she was a migrant who spoke little English. It was nearly Christmas, which made finding work even harder.

Finally, she came to a factory where they employed lots of migrant women. At last! The factory made tiny parts for radios and other electronic devices, and the foreman told her to come back in the morning, ready for work.

The rules were strict. Workers couldn't even go to the toilet without a supervisor, and there was no talking on the factory floor. They made sure of this by putting women who spoke different languages side by side.

The work was fiddly and reminded Gisela of the sewing classes she'd hated at school. She had to fuse a tiny wire to a metal contraption under a microscope using tweezers. Two hundred and fifty an hour was the goal. While she was learning how to do it, she felt clumsy and slow. It was incredible to watch the more experienced women at work – they soldered the wire so quickly that Gisela could hardly see their hands move.

*

Life was moving so fast. Gisela tried not to let everything that was new overwhelm her.

Thinking back to her childhood – having a stutter and being bullied at school – every day had seemed impossible, but she'd got through one problem after another. She'd survived the hunger and neglect of her early years. She'd emerged strong and positive. Even being called 'scum' by girls at school hadn't stopped her. The newness of Australia wasn't going to stop her either.

The next weekend after getting the job, Gisela and her daughter were invited to a neighbourhood barbecue. Gisela was relieved that she had understood what the woman was saying, though she was confused about the instruction to 'bring a plate'. Didn't her neighbour have enough plates to host the meal? In Germany that would be a strange thing to ask a guest to do.

When Saturday came, the woman opened the door, Gisela smiled and handed her a clean plate. The woman looked puzzled but invited them inside.

The food was laid out in the garden – sausages (though she was sure the man called them *snags*) and rissoles, potato salad, sliced tomatoes on crisp lettuce, and a cabbage salad. Even if barbecuing was new to her, this food seemed a little familiar at least.

There were some stranger items such as half an orange speared with toothpicks, with a piece of cheese and a tiny onion on the end of each one. But there were plenty of plates for everyone, which made Gisela wonder why she had been asked to bring one.

After the meal, when she'd said her thanks and was leaving, the neighbour handed Gisela her clean plate, which hadn't been used. Gisela still couldn't understand this mysterious ritual.

At home she telephoned a new friend, who spoke a bit of German, to tell her about the 'bring a plate' experience.

'Dear Gisela!' Her friend burst out laughing. 'Bring a plate doesn't *literally* mean bring a plate. It means bring a dish of food for everyone to share at the party!'

'Oh, no!' Gisela felt deeply ashamed of her mistake. What on earth must have gone through her neighbour's mind when Gisela handed over an empty plate at the door? 'How can I ever show my face again?'

'Listen,' said her friend, 'there's an Australian phrase you need to know: *no worries*. It means forget about it, Gisela. Don't be so hard on yourself.'

That made her feel better. Gisela dreaded mistakes like that, but eventually, she saw the funny side.

8

Bush magic

It was six o'clock in the morning and Gisela was making breakfast so that she'd be on time for the 7 a.m. clock-in at the factory. With the back door open she could hear the song of the large black-and-white bird that sat on the roof. Gisela knew by now that they were called magpies. There were magpies in Germany but they weren't like these bigger birds with a long, pale beak that had a dark tip. Australian magpies were striking singers. They were making a deep, fluty sound that Gisela loved.

At the factory, Gisela worked in silence with the fine wires and tweezers. She still hadn't managed to reach the goal of 250 pieces per hour and the stress was rising. What if they thought she was too slow? What if she lost her job? It had been hard enough to find this one.

Each day at four o'clock after she arrived home, Gisela turned on the television for another episode of *Marine Boy* to improve her English. Afterwards, she cooked supper, played with her daughter, bathed her and put her to bed.

Then it was time for night school.

It took more than an hour to get there, but even on the train journey Gisela was busy; she'd realised that her English lessons with *Marine Boy* were not enough. Day to day she spent so much time asking people to speak slowly or to spell things. She needed a faster method of learning, so she was trying a new technique: the Schliemann Method. This meant that she had to learn, off by heart, the first thirty pages of a book written in English. She wasn't allowed to look up the words, she had to memorise every sentence in a language that was foreign to her. Only once this was mastered could she look up the words.

At night school, Gisela listened and took notes as best she could. And afterwards, she stood at the train station, nervous to be on her own in the dark in a city that still seemed new.

Home at last, Gisela listened as the friend who'd looked after Peta all evening tried to discourage her from this hectic life.

'You don't even speak proper English, Gisela, how will you pass exams? Look at you, you're so tired!'

The friend was right about one thing, Gisela *was* exhausted. The following day, she collapsed in the factory and the doctor's diagnosis was stress. Something had to change. Still, she would not give up on her studies. There had to be another way to raise her daughter, pay the bills and get her qualifications.

She thought of Nan and the stones in the river. The stones were a kind of magic – the kind you had to look out for, or you'd miss them.

*

The next Sunday, Gisela took her daughter to a church group that had been recommended to her. She had started to feel loneliness creep in. It was so difficult to build a community when you were

71

new to a country. She felt she could ignore the discrimination that she experienced because of her accent and slowly improving English if she made new friends.

Some of the people at church admired her for coming to Australia with a child but no husband. Although she was much too proud to tell them about how hard it was to pay her bills on factory wages, there was good advice on offer.

'You're wrung out from working in that factory,' said a woman she got chatting to over a cup of tea. 'Why don't you become a driving instructor, like I am? It's a flexible job and better money. People will tell you that women can't teach people to drive, but you learn to ignore them.'

This sounded perfect. Gisela had always loved driving. As soon as she discovered that there was a theory test, she started to learn the entire instruction manual off by heart. After all, she was not yet confident enough to answer in English sentences. And if anyone could memorise a whole manual, it was Gisela.

By the time the driving instructor test came around, Gisela knew the whole book. She rattled off every answer, hardly drawing breath, and passed the exams as well as the driving test on her first go.

This stone in the river would pay for Gisela's studies for the next ten years.

*

'Are you interested in art?' another new friend asked her at the church group. 'I'm part of a group that meets in the mountains where artists gather to paint and talk. You should come.'

Gisela thought back to the teacher who'd taken her to art galleries in Berlin in the days when school had been a battlefield.

She had not felt the urge to paint since she'd arrived in Australia, especially as the landscape she'd seen so far looked harsh, without the colours she was used to. In one way, Australia had felt like home from the moment she'd arrived, but in another it was a country she didn't understand. Perhaps it was so vast and different from Germany that she never would.

Soon after, Gisela drove with some church group members to an old, rambling house in the Dandenong Ranges, a lush, green set of low mountain ranges just outside Melbourne's eastern suburbs. The place was brimming with people and paintings. Gisela's friend pointed out all the local and visiting artists as they walked around.

By now, Gisela's English was good enough for friendly conversation, thanks to *Marine Boy* and the Schliemann Method. She got talking to an artist called Ronald Bull. He had masses of shiny black hair and wore a beautiful velvet jacket. Ron was kind and reserved and they shared the same sense of humour. Gisela found him easy to get along with and they swapped life stories.

> The Gunai/Kurnai people are the traditional owners of Gippsland in south-eastern Australia. Between 1910 and the 1970s, many First Nations' children were forcibly removed from their families because of government policies.

Ronald Bull was a Gunai man and a member of the Stolen Generation. The government had taken him away from his family twice as a child. The first time, he was four months old. When he was twelve, he was taken again and sent to Tally Ho Boys' Training Farm to attend school and be a farm labourer, and at 15 he was fostered in Melbourne.

Ron's life was hard, and he'd been in and out of prison since he was a teenager. Along the way he'd studied with artists and taught himself to paint. He was now an up-and-coming landscape artist who was earning respect in the art world.

From then on Gisela attended the art group once a month. At one of the meetings, Ron said, 'I've got a great spot I want to paint next weekend. Do you want to come?'

'I can drive us there,' she suggested.

A week later, Gisela and Ron came to the spot he'd talked about. As Ron set up his easel, Gisela looked out at the landscape he planned to paint. It was her first time deep in the bush, which looked so different from the forests she'd grown up with. She couldn't understand why Ron had chosen this place. To her, it didn't look special enough for a painting.

After a few hours, Gisela asked if she could peek at the canvas. As she looked from Ron's painting to the landscape, back and forth a few more times, she felt something shift inside. The view she'd thought of as plain was magically transformed. The light and colour that Ron had captured made her see how beautiful and unique the bush was. It felt as if he'd flicked a switch and changed her connection to the place.

To Gisela it was a huge privilege to look at the land through Ron's painting. This artist had shown her a new way of seeing, and it marked the beginning of Gisela feeling at home in the Australian bush.

*

In 1969, Gisela's friend was driving her to the centre of Melbourne to get her results from *The Age* headquarters. Every year, just after midnight on a set day in December, the newspaper published the final high school exam results of every student in Victoria. Gisela's young daughter was asleep in the back of the car.

Everything rested on these results. All that hard work: getting to know Australian customs, learning English, attending night school, working full-time and raising a child. If Gisela failed, she didn't have enough money to take the exams again.

'Can't you go a bit faster?' she said.

Her friend smiled, noticing Gisela's fidgety legs bobbing up and down.

She couldn't relax. The mid-year exams had been a disaster. After studying hard for them, she'd blinked in disbelief when she received her results: 33%. Fail. What had gone wrong? A British woman had walked past then and, noticing the devastation on Gisela's face, peered over her shoulder. 'You poor dear,' she'd remarked, in a haughty tone, 'you'll never make it'. Gisela hated to be pitied.

Her history teacher had put things into perspective.

'You knew the right things,' he'd said, 'the trouble is you wrote it in all the wrong boxes'.

If you didn't put the answer in the right box, you scored zero no matter how much correct information you'd written elsewhere. It was a different system from exams she'd sat back in Germany and Gisela hadn't known what to expect.

Since then she had done lots of practice exams, improved her English and studied even harder. The final exams had been held a few weeks ago in the Great Hall of the grand Exhibition Building during one of Melbourne's heatwaves. Over 40 degrees each day. Hundreds of small tables in a large space with no air-conditioning.

Gisela's friend parked the car opposite the headquarters of *The Age*. It was a large building of severe brown bricks and there were thousands of students milling around outside. Each exam paper had only a number to identify the student. Now she had to look for that number in the results supplement.

'Here they come,' said her friend.

Men arrived with large piles of newspapers and placed them on the pavement outside the building. Gisela managed to duck into the crowds to grab one. The printed numbers were tiny, so together they scanned down the columns under the streetlight.

'My number isn't here!' Gisela said in a panic.

All around her, students yelled with relief or quietly walked to a corner to let the bad news sink in.

She and her friend kept searching each subject, Gisela feeling more frantic when her student number didn't appear.

'Have you checked the scholarship page?' asked a man who worked at the paper and noted her dismay. It hadn't occurred to Gisela to look under scholarships, the awards for the highest-scoring students.

But there it was, her number! A scholarship for excellence! She hadn't just passed the exams, she'd aced them.

'So, what now?' her friend asked as they celebrated. 'What will you study? What career do you want?'

Gisela looked up at the wide night, an Australian sky filled with stars. She hadn't known any of these constellations as a child in the northern hemisphere. They stretched in all directions, like the possibilities she could imagine now.

9

The Professor

Professor Gisela Kaplan read the sign on the door.

It was 20 years since that night in Melbourne. Gisela had chosen to study literature, sociology and psychology at university. After she had completed her first degree, she was advised to study a Diploma of Education to become a high school teacher. That was the career women were often directed into in the 1970s. Some people even thought that women didn't have the kind of brains to do well at maths and science. They were discouraged from going in other directions.

Once Gisela completed her Bachelor of Arts (BA), she was awarded *another* scholarship. So, she stayed on at university and completed a Master of Arts (MA) followed by a PhD, which made her Dr Kaplan. Not a doctor who could take out your tonsils but a doctor who'd studied literature and human society. And now she was a Professor of Social Sciences, a teacher of the highest rank in a university.

A BA usually takes 3 years, and an MA took 2 years at that time. The PhD (Doctor of Philosophy) is a research degree that takes about 4 years of full-time work, in addition.

Her studies had been devoted to social injustice and racism. She'd written six books and many articles. Her daughter was an adult by now, with her own family. Gisela had moved to Brisbane, which she'd had to do without her life partner, Lesley, whom she'd met at university. The sign on Lesley's door said **Professor Lesley Rogers** and she specialised in brain development and animal behaviour at a university in New South Wales.

Gisela was happy with her life and in what she was doing at work. Although in some ways she felt like an outsider in Australia, it was not the same as being an outsider as a child in Berlin. It was a feeling she could enjoy.

Then one day, Lesley rang Gisela's office to tell her some news.

'I've been invited to a neuroscience conference in Europe,' she said. 'Would you like to come with me?'

'I'd love to! I'll book the flights,' Gisela replied. She called the travel agent that day to make the arrangements.

'It's a long flight to Europe,' said the travel agent. 'Would you like to do any stops along the way? It's currently $200 to stop off in Borneo, if that's of interest to you.'

Borneo, the largest island in Asia and one of the most diverse places on earth for animals, birds and plants. A century ago, Borneo had been covered in lush rainforest but that had started to be destroyed at an alarming rate. A quarter of it had gone already because of deforestation.

A diverse population of animals live there, including orangutans, pygmy elephants and clouded leopards.

Gisela thought back to the days of the mobile library in Berlin and how she'd loved the stories of the jungle written by Rudyard Kipling. There was *The Jungle Book*, of course, and the *Just So* stories about how animals came to look the way they do. She remembered *How the Leopard Got His Spots* and *How the Elephant Got His Trunk*.

Suddenly there was nothing she wanted to do more than stop off in Borneo to explore the jungle. If only she could convince Lesley.

*

The plane approached over Mount Kinabalu, the highest mountain in Malaysia. Even from up here, Gisela and Lesley could see from the vibrant green why Mount Kinabalu was one of the richest places in the world for flora and fauna. After landing, they headed for the Sepilok Rehabilitation Centre not far from the town of Sandakan.

The Centre opened in 1964 to provide a sanctuary for orangutans,

> The size of the rainforest that the Centre covers is 43 sq km, roughly the same as 2,000 sports stadiums like the MCG.

whose existence was threatened by logging and poaching. Many were orphaned.

Accompanied by a guide, they set off to explore. Gisela didn't like to admit it but she was nervous. She'd spent her childhood in Berlin, travelled from city to city in Europe as a budding opera singer, and had lived in two more cities since moving to Australia: she was a city dweller and this was very different territory. The rainforest was teeming with life but not as she knew it. Not with people and cars and busy avenues of shops, theatres and galleries but with the kind of wildlife and terrain that had fascinated adventurous types for centuries.

It was humid, the air hot and damp. Sweat was running down her face and stinging her eyes. Right now, she could be in a fancy air-conditioned hotel in Paris but instead she was calculating the odds of bumping into one of Borneo's less friendly inhabitants. Bloodsuckers like leeches and mosquitos, two-metre-long water monitors, sun bears that dwelled in trees and weighed 70 kilos,

> The **sun bear** has a long tongue – up to 25 cm – which is used to extract honey from beehives.

84

bearded pigs, saltwater crocodiles, and 24 kinds of venomous snake.

Gisela and Lesley stood in a clearing. With caution, a young orangutan approached them, and the guide said, 'This is Abbie. An orphan. She's three years old.'

Abbie had witnessed the murder of her mother by poachers. It was the aim of the Centre to keep her safe and well-fed while she was young and to teach her how to find food and how to climb. In orangutan society, the mother is everything to her baby: food, comfort, safety and travel. Young orangutans cling to their mother's fur when she climbs trees or swings or walks across the rainforest floor.

Pongo pygmaeus is the scientific name for orangutans.

With the exception of humans, orangutans spend more time raising their children than any other primate species. Young orangutans develop slowly under their mother's watchful eye, learning everything from her. So when an orangutan is orphaned they have as much hope of surviving alone as a human child.

Abbie watched Gisela for a few moments. Then in a swift move she crawled up Gisela's body as if she were a small tree. She came around her side and got comfortable on Gisela's hip with her long arms around Gisela's neck. Perplexed, Gisela wrapped her arms around the orangutan.

It seemed too magical for words. Abbie nuzzled her neck and clung on tightly.

'What do I do now?' Gisela whispered to Lesley.

'I don't think you've got much choice in the matter,' she replied. 'She's not going to let you go!'

Gisela's mother had always insisted that animals smelled bad and carried germs. But as Gisela breathed in Abbie's scent, she was surprised: the smell was citrusy, like orange peel. Abbie's skin was delicate and velvety, not taut like a child's skin but soft like that of an older person.

This semi-wild creature seemed to trust Gisela. She thought back to the night at the circus: the lion tamer who'd said that he'd never seen lions respond so calmly to a stranger.

For hours she carried Abbie around – all ten kilograms of her. Eventually, she had to sit down on a log. Still as close as could be, they studied each

other's hands. Abbie had fine fingers, which she ran across the lines on Gisela's palm. She mimicked sounds Gisela made and watched her face with deep curiosity.

When it came time to go, Gisela and Lesley had a feeling that leaving Abbie behind would not go smoothly. Sure enough, when the guide untangled Abbie's limbs from around Gisela's waist and neck, the orphan orangutan began to scream. It was worse than Gisela could have imagined. Abbie's voice was as full of fear and desperation as a terrified child calling for her mother. Why had she let Abbie get so attached to her when she knew their time together would be brief? The guide tried everything to calm Abbie down but she continued to shriek in distress and reach out for Gisela. Having no other choice, Gisela walked away feeling devastated, guilty and foolish.

Of all the languages that Gisela had managed to learn in her lifetime, this experience in the

> Facial expressions are an important form of communication in orangutans. They also communicate with gestures and a variety of calls.

rainforest had shown her that there was another kind of language that she was destined for: animal communication. That day in Berlin Zoo with Nan, Gisela had felt such a powerful desire to help the fox. It had taken many years and another unique connection with a wild animal to remember that feeling. Now she could do something about it.

10

Curiosity

'Am I doing the right thing?' Gisela asked Lesley.

'Changing direction in your forties, for an orangutan?' replied Lesley with a wry smile. 'Does it feel like the right thing?'

Gisela thought for a moment. 'It does,' she said. 'Our trip has changed things.'

'Or it reminded you of something that was always there.'

Back home in Queensland, Gisela applied for a research grant to study primates – and persuaded Lesley, who worked at another university, to put her name to the grant as well. Primates can mean any mammal in two sub-orders: the prosimians (lemurs, lorises and tarsiers) and the anthropoids (monkeys, apes, and humans).

The evidence of primates as forest-dwellers exists in fossils that date to the Late Cretaceous period (97.5 to 66.4 million years ago). It was an English naturalist, Charles Darwin in 1859, who concluded that humans and great apes have a common ancestor.

Gisela already had a degree in psychology – the science of how humans think, feel, behave and learn. Now she would shift her focus to studying those same things in great apes and perhaps even other primates, starting with the endangered Bornean orangutan.

*

As they lived and worked in different cities, Gisela and Lesley talked about their plans on the phone.

'It would be fantastic if we got the grant,' said Lesley. 'Nobody has done this work in wild or re-habilitating orangutans before.'

They had applied for funds to study handedness in orangutans, which means looking to see whether wild orangutans use a preferred hand in certain tasks, like humans do.

Lesley knew what an important role handedness plays in brain studies. It's to do with how the brain is divided into right and left sides (or hemispheres). Each side controls particular behaviours. Lesley had done a lot of laboratory work on the brains of chicks. She was the first scientist in the world to prove that an animal's brain processes visual information differently on the left and right sides, just as a human brain does.

> Approximately 90% of humans are right-handed.

This was an important discovery. It disproved the belief that humans are the only species with a brain that works in that way, which disproved the idea that this made humans unique in relation to other animals.

'I'd also like to use the time to find out some basic information about the way orangutans communicate,' said Gisela. 'They're meant to be amongst our closest relatives but we know next to nothing about their way of thinking and acting.'

The exciting part was that they would do their research in the very home of orangutans, not in zoos, not in the western world, but directly in Borneo. This is what is known as 'fieldwork'. At that time, very few scientists had done such fieldwork, and nobody from Australia had.

Borneo was a spectacular place but also very dangerous. Along with the unbearable heat, it was not an environment for the faint-hearted.

If they got the grant, they would observe the orangutans from a distance. No matter how much of a magical experience it had been with Abbie, their role as scientists was to study the species methodically and with minimal interference. So little was known about their behaviour. What did they do all day? Which forest food was on their menu? Where did they sleep? Did they have friends, a social network?

Most scientific research is funded by government grants, or non-profit organisations, or companies.

Gisela and Lesley made a long list of questions about orangutan society and a daily plan for how they would conduct their research.

*

It took two years of dedicated work and grant applications, but finally they were on their way.

Mount Kinabalu's peak was shrouded in heavy rain clouds. As they stepped off the plane, Gisela was reminded that one of the challenges of fieldwork in Borneo was the weather. She was already sweating and brushing insects from her skin.

Once inside the rehabilitation centre, the challenges of the forest multiplied. It was a hot, sticky heat, with no wind to soothe the skin. Gisela and Lesley's equipment suffered in the humidity – binoculars went fuzzy, batteries expired quickly, and the zoom lenses on their cameras had trouble focusing. It was vital to record their observations with great accuracy so Gisela spent more time fanning the video camera than her roasting hot face. She even put her hat on it when it was not in use to shield it from the burning sun.

Gisela's main enemy were the forest bloodsuckers: mosquitoes, elephant flies, sandflies, ticks and leeches. The usual insect repellents were no use in the jungle because of the degree of sweat on their skin. So they wore army jungle clothes, with cloth thick enough that mosquitoes could not get in. It made them even hotter but it was the better option compared to the dangers of malaria. On top of that they wore a photographer's vest, woollen socks and heavy army boots.

On day one, Gisela let out a loud scream when she discovered a leech engorged on her belly. It was thumb-sized with orange and black stripes. She dabbed some salt on its mouth and it immediately let go, but the sight and feel of it was hard to forget.

Their days of observing and recording continued. Orangutans tend to wander and may travel several kilometres in search of food. When they're uncomfortable with being watched, or feel threatened, they climb higher into the forest canopy, which can be 20 metres and even higher from the ground.

In fieldwork, it is important to watch closely but to allow animals to continue with their normal daily activities without interference.
The slow process of making animals feel comfortable with the presence of a particular person is called habituation.

Their nests for resting at night made of branches and leaves are typically high in the canopy too. Challenges such as these were among the reasons that there were so few studies of wild and semi-wild orangutans. And this deepened Gisela and Lesley's commitment to their research.

One day, Gisela was alone when she found herself surrounded by another type of primate: a troop of 30 macaques. Amongst them were seven young males spearheading the troop. Judging by their body language, Gisela could tell that they meant trouble and could do her harm – perhaps for a dare or to prove themselves to the rest of the troop. After all, she was in their territory. The sharp teeth and malicious stance of these seven aggressive young males could be real danger. They could maul and even kill her. She had no weapons, not even a stick.

Gisela had to think of something quickly. Running would be a mistake because they would outrun her. She knew some monkey facial signals: mouth stretched open baring the top row of teeth was not a smile but a threat display. As her teeth weren't as big as those of the macaques, they might see that as weakness so she needed to add something else to it – a sound, perhaps? All Gisela could think of was a hissing noise like a snake or water monitor.

Once they were close enough she used three signals: she stood firm and tried to look confident (not that she felt it), then she bared her teeth and hissed loudly. As if by magic, the troop scattered at speed! Luckily, she had judged the situation well and the combination of signals had convinced the monkeys that this trespasser had more defences than they thought.

Her heart still thumping, Gisela noted that tuning into macaque society had saved her from an attack.

Overcoming every challenge put to them, Gisela and Lesley's research trip was successful and they brought back significant new data on the handedness of orangutans in their natural environment. They observed that, like wild gorillas, orangutans as a group don't use one hand dominantly for feeding, but that they show a left-hand preference for fine motor skills around their faces such as cleaning their eyes, ears or teeth. Findings like this led to further visits to Borneo.

*

Two years later, in the late afternoon when most staff had left the rehabilitation centre, Gisela set up their camera tripod in a clearing. Finding a safe place to sit down, she took in the bird calls, the small glimpses of sky, and the way the heat cocooned her. A soft mist was descending from the tops of the trees.

In the distance, an orangutan approached, dropping in and out of view because of the dense foliage.

'This could be Abbie,' said Lesley, quietly. They could not be sure how this encounter would go. Gisela stayed where she was, very still.

Gradually, the orangutan made her way towards them. Although she'd grown and changed a lot,

Gisela hoped that it was her because in that reserve juvenile orangutans rarely approached humans in such a direct way.

Abbie got closer, remaining watchful and alert. Gisela tried not to stare or make sudden movements.

It was a once-in-a-lifetime moment as Abbie sat down in front of Gisela. The orangutan took her hand, turned it palm facing up and ran her index finger along the lines. Gisela and Lesley had observed the same type of interaction between infant orangutans and their mothers.

After sitting still for some time, Abbie got up and disappeared, returning soon after with a young female around the same age as her. The two of them appeared to be friends and played together while Gisela and Lesley watched.

As dusk fell, Abbie came close to Gisela again and held her hand for a moment. Then she let go and slowly disappeared into the depths of the jungle. For Gisela, it was another moment of awe.

*

On Gisela and Lesley's next trip to Borneo, Abbie had adopted a little boy orangutan – Tom – whose mother had been killed by poachers just like Abbie's had. Tom clung to Abbie for the whole visit, so terrified of being separated from her that he would shriek if she turned away from him. So it was evidence of great trust when Abbie brought Tom to meet Gisela.

By now, Gisela understood a lot about orangutan communication. She knew how important it was to treat Tom as a wild animal, not to try to humanise him. Survival in the jungle depended on it, among other factors.

This time, Abbie did not take Gisela's hand or touch her at all, but stayed close by, looking at her. After this quiet contemplation, Abbie swung from the woody vines, performed somersaults and pulled a face that Gisela recognised as 'playing'. Abbie had grown into a strong and capable adult who was now taking great care of a juvenile.

Other young semi-wild orangutans approached them at the rehab centre in addition to Abbie. One of them climbed up the tripod as if it were a tree. Another took hold of Lesley's pencil and ran away with it. When Gisela felt something tugging on the pocket of her khaki waistcoat, she turned to find a long arm extending from it and a young orangutan rooting around to see what was inside.

These funny sights had a more worrying side to them: the demand for nature-based holidays meant that more and more tourists were coming to centres like this, and as a result the orangutans had lost their fear of humans and had become quite cheeky, and even dangerous.

By now, Gisela and Lesley had enough to write their first book about Bornean orangutans.

They had observed the behaviour, diet, parent-infant bonds, vocalisation and handedness of over 50 orangutans during their trips, and recorded 250 hours on tape for close study back at home.

The orangutans they watched had eaten dozens of different plants (including mango, durian, lychee and fig) as well as proteins (from worms to small birds and lizards). Their vocalisation included distress calls, such as the 'soft hoot' of young animals when they are worried, and a threat call known as 'chomping' where the animal forces the lower jaw upwards and makes a gulp in the presence of an intruder.

Also among their observations was the diversity of the species: facial features as well as personalities.

Out of all the great apes, it's only orangutans that have the same skin colour variations as humans do.

Having learned how vital the forest is for the survival of this very special ape, in the epilogue of their book Gisela and Lesley wrote passionately against the destruction of the lowlands in Borneo for human settlement, agriculture and logging.

11

Orphans

Mid-Spring in Armidale, in the Northern Tablelands of New South Wales, and the early morning air was cool. It was 1993 and Gisela had come a long way from the young woman who'd left Germany with a baby daughter and a few suitcases. Outdoors on their sprawling property, Gisela and Lesley were having breakfast to celebrate Gisela's birthday.

On their five acres they kept a donkey, a few sheep who produced excellent wool that they sold each year, fruit trees, and a huge vegetable garden where they grew bok choy, beetroot, pumpkins and sweetcorn along with many others, depending on the season. After the desperate hunger of her childhood, Gisela took joy in growing her own produce and making delicious jams and marmalade.

A stream of birds flitted in the shrubbery and trees seeking breakfasts of their own: Eastern spinebills, galahs, magpies, currawongs, superb fairy-wrens. At this time of day the chorus sounded like twenty different conversations, as if the birds were shopping in a busy fruit and veg market. Who knew if one species ever spoke to another or if they only whistled and trilled to their own kind?

Their dog, Tipsy, paid the birds no attention. He was a Rhodesian Ridgeback*, part of the family since Lesley had helped Gisela to get over her childhood phobia of dogs that had made life difficult for years. Before meeting Lesley, Gisela couldn't even walk down a street if she saw a dog. She'd start to shake and would hurry away in the other direction.

But Lesley had always had a dog and she'd been determined to help Gisela get over her fears. By explaining dog behaviour so that Gisela understood each gesture or bark, and by not making her rush into anything she wasn't ready for, Lesley helped Gisela's fear to gradually fall away. Ever since then, Gisela got on well with dogs and she loved Tipsy.

Born into a litter of thirteen, Tipsy had been one of the smallest pups, but she had a white tip on her tail that made her stand out from the crowd. Tipsy had chosen Gisela the first time they'd met – by now Gisela was used to being adopted by animals.

Birthdays aside, Gisela and Lesley both had to work that day. There were lectures and seminars to give at the university, and they also had to tend to their colony of common marmosets, a species of small monkey from Brazil. In Australia there was a freeze on research permits to Borneo, so all of their current primatology work was in the lab. But thanks to Gisela and Lesley, the University of New England was about the only place in Australia at that time where primate behaviour could be studied on campus and at the highest level.

This work was about the brain function of primates. The more they could learn about how animals thought and what they felt, the more hope there was of influencing positive change in human behaviour, such as our impact on the environment and our approach to public zoos. Gisela and Lesley felt strongly that orangutans were unsuited to confinement.

Long-term captivity can significantly stress wildlife and result in depression, behavioural problems and loss of survival skills.

'I hope you enjoy this birthday gift,' said Lesley, sliding an envelope across the table. Inside was an invitation to a wildlife rehabilitation* course. Gisela could choose which species of animal to be trained in. 'As we can't go to the jungle at the moment, your natural way with animals could be put to use right here.'

Gisela's face lit up. 'This is perfect, Lesley!'

'When you pass the course, you can apply for a licence to rehabilitate local wildlife. I remember how much I enjoyed hand-raising a southern hairy-nosed wombat when I was a teenager in South Australia. They're shy, sensitive creatures, vulnerable to climate change. Or you could choose wallabies or kangaroo joeys, orphaned by bushfires and car accidents.'

Lesley cleared the breakfast things and went inside but Gisela sat for a while, soaking up the morning sun and birdsong. Tipsy was wrestling a large stick. What would Tipsy do if their property were suddenly filled with orphaned joeys? Would she see the joeys as playmates? Rhodesian Ridgebacks like to play rough, and Gisela didn't want to spend the days telling off her dog for doing what came naturally. Nor could she bear to think about a joey being injured under her care, or joeys losing their fear of dogs and then, after release, getting killed by wild dogs because they had not learned to flee.

Lesley came back out. 'Have you decided which animal yet?'

'I think so. What about an aviary just here?' Gisela replied, sketching the shape and size of it in the air.

'An aviary? You're going to rehabilitate *birds*?' Lesley said. 'What about the joeys?'

'No good with the dog. Birds it is.'

'But Gisela, what do you know about birds?'

'Almost nothing!' she replied. 'I used to have a pet budgie called Perle but that's about it. Nothing like a pair of fresh eyes on a subject, don't you think?'

'I suppose so…' Lesley's brows knitted together. 'But do we really want agitated magpies flapping all over the place?'

'Don't worry about a thing!' said Gisela. 'The birds will be out here in aviaries until they're ready to be released into the wild. You and Tipsy will hardly notice them.'

*

Soon the backyard in Armidale looked very different. Gisela built not one but several shelters to house all the different species, including large-flight aviaries specifically designed for songbirds and parrots, and strong intensive-care aviaries for birds of prey.

She could not have known then how many birds would be coming and going over the next 20 years. Juvenile magpies whose parents had been killed, a young tawny frogmouth who had lost the ability to hunt, a shy Eastern rosella with hardly any feathers, an elderly galah who had a fear of baseball caps, a sulphur-crested cockatoo who liked nothing better than to be showered with the garden hose. And hundreds of species she had never even seen before. All those and many more were to come.

Birds had captivated Gisela since she'd taken the course. Her new hobby occupied every minute she could spare. She was fast becoming the Bird Lady of Armidale. People brought injured or orphaned birds to the house, expecting her magic touch. Truck drivers passing through Armidale on night deliveries left sick birds they'd found by the roadside in shoeboxes on Gisela's doorstep.

One evening, Gisela was holding a young tawny frogmouth who'd been brought to her with head injuries. Through weeks of observation, she'd come to realise that this sweet bird had brain damage. He could no longer recognise food and had to be fed like a nestling*. When Gisela tapped his beak, he would open up. He then clamped the mouse she fed him, the tail hanging out like a piece of spaghetti. This was the only way to keep him nourished.

She would need to apply for special permission to keep this tawny in her garden aviary permanently. Though healthy in every other way, he would never survive alone without the ability to hunt. Her licence to rescue and rehabilitate birds depended on a promise to release them into the wild as soon as they were well enough. If that wasn't possible, the bird should be euthanised. But Gisela was persuasive. She'd find a way.

Although she was very busy with her work in primatology, writing new research papers and teaching

> Gisela obtained the permit and this tawny frogmouth is still alive in 2021, 27 years later.

at the university, caring for and communicating with birds quickly began to feel like Gisela's destiny.

*

Gisela opened the door of the aviary one day and held a larva in her fingertips. The baby bird opened her beak hungrily. She was a young, orphaned magpie – Billie – barely a few weeks old.

This wasn't going to be an easy job. Magpie parenting was intensive and lasted for months. Billie could not fly yet and had no idea how to find and recognise food. To live in the wild she would need to be given survival skills. Right now Billie was completely dependent on adult care.

At dawn, Gisela foraged in the garden for the correct breakfast. Feeding a magpie human food like minced meat would leave it malnourished, and it would not tell the bird what to look for in the wild. Accompanied by a curious Tipsy, Gisela dug up worms and turned over rocks to look for slater bugs. She peeled small pieces of bark from the trees to find insects, and peered among the firewood logs, careful not to upset venomous spiders that might be lurking. If she was going to be a good carer for this baby bird and eventually set her free, she'd have to stay true to what its parents would have done, at least as far as a human could.

'Are you sure about this?' said Lesley, bringing out a cup of tea for Gisela. 'She'll need months of feeding. And then there's her socialisation to consider.'

Gisela had no doubts about the commitment. At the same time as she was feeding nestlings, including Billie, every half hour, or giving birds medicine or injections, applying bandages, even performing minor surgery, she had her career as a scientist to maintain. She was working on a complex scientific paper about primates, had lecture notes to prepare, a chapter of a book to write, as well as university students to supervise in their laboratory work. Then there were essays to mark, scientific trials to run, and over 100 emails a day to reply to.

Sleep? She slept like a bird: with one half of her brain still awake.

It reminded her of the early days in Melbourne when she had a toddler, a factory job, night school, a language to learn and a new country to adapt to. Only this time she was driven not by the need to survive but by her passion. Those words of Nan's still rang in her ears: *if you have hope and determination, that is all you need.*

As Billie the magpie grew, she walked beside Gisela all over the five-acre property. In this way Gisela was able to show her where the best insects were hiding so that one day Billie could look for them on her own. She was learning just as much as Billie. Billie pulled Gisela's shoelaces, hung upside down on the hills hoist, ran victoriously through the garden when she'd snatched a dog toy, and rolled around on the ground as if waiting for a tickle.

Australian birds can form alliances in cases of danger. For example, noisy miners may help magpies when an eagle or goshawk intrudes into their territories.

Gisela was learning that Australian magpies are curious, affectionate, intelligent and very playful.

113

The same could be said of most cockatoos, including galahs, as well as ravens, from what she had seen. There was so much more to these birds than she'd imagined. Was it something about Australia, she wondered, that made these birds remarkable?

Like many people, Gisela had taken birds for granted in the past, but not any more. What didn't we know about these birds? What *should* we know? And as a scientist, what could Gisela discover and pass on?

*

It was late afternoon and Gisela was alone in the house when she suddenly heard: 'I've got dinner for you!'

Who'd said that?

'Hello?' she called out in confusion.

'I've got dinner for you!' the voice repeated.

What on earth, she thought. Gisela went outside and approached Billie's aviary. She waited, and waited, but all was quiet.

Lesley was the one in the house who liked to cook: had the magpie learnt these particular words by overhearing Lesley speak?

Gisela set up a recorder next to Billie's aviary. It was not long before she'd captured the magpie saying the words again: *I've got dinner for you!* She was stunned. So it was true, Billie had learnt some of Lesley's human words. Her first question was: why had the magpie copied Lesley when Gisela was the main caregiver?

She wanted to know what else Billie could say. There was no doubt that magpies were amongst the best songbirds in the world. They had so many different sounds, songs and calls. That loud, flute-like, complex song that went *wardle-ordle-ardle-ardle-ordle!* was fascinating. What else could she discover about their vocalisation*?

Gisela's rehabilitation work naturally led to her reading books and journals about Australian birds, which she discovered are some of the most interesting in the world. In 2004 it was finally confirmed that all songbirds first evolved in Australia. Many Australian ornithologists* had suspected this for years but needed proof. Now they had it from genetic studies of songbirds and parrots.

The long history of Australian birds became central to Gisela's studies. The British Empire, which colonised the land that came to be known as Australia from 1788, had misunderstood Australian wildlife. At the time, people in the northern hemisphere believed that the most exciting animals, birds and plant-life came from Europe. This prompted European settlers to introduce many species to Australia, such as rabbits, foxes, carp, starlings, Indian mynahs, blackberries and prickly pears. But introduced species caused huge environmental problems. Now it had been scientifically proven that Australian flora and fauna were unique in terms of evolution*.

Sixty-five million years ago, an asteroid, 12 kilometres wide, crashed into the ocean near Mexico with such force that it sent shockwaves around the world. Clouds of particles darkened the skies for years. Plants died, dinosaurs died, in fact so did most life on Earth. Miraculously, some bird species survived, hidden away in pockets of East Gondwana, or what we now call Australia. Once the skies became clear and the sunlight could reach the earth again, the surviving birds developed over millions of years into many species.

Gisela was struck by the significance of Australian birds and their long history. Australian birds were more intelligent, resourceful and more emotional than most people realised.

Besides being a rescuer, Gisela couldn't help observing her birds like the scientist she was. Since the experience of hearing Billie speak human words, she felt compelled to redirect her scientific research from primates to birds, and from international to local wildlife. She really felt she had no choice! From now on she would pour all of her curiosity and conviction into birds – starting with magpies.

What began as a thoughtful birthday present from Lesley was about to change Gisela's life.

12

Fieldwork

It wasn't easy to be a female scientist in a male-dominated career, and most people don't start to learn a completely new branch of science in later life. But Gisela was not put off by either one of these concerns.

No matter what the consequences would be, she decided to enrol in another PhD, this time at the Veterinary School at Queensland University. She was going to study Australian magpies' vocal development and the ways they communicate.

To do this, Gisela would need to record thousands of hours of magpie observation. And that meant one thing: fieldwork.

Eager to begin, Gisela packed her car at dawn on a warm, windless morning: camcorder, long-distance microphone, sound amplifier, binoculars, camera, and the most trusted piece of equipment for a field research scientist: a notebook and pencil. She headed out of Armidale into the Northern Tablelands, the largest highland area in Australia. Before colonisation, the diverse wildlife had co-existed with the Anaywan people of the First Nations.

To choose research sites for her observations, Gisela had to work out which area of land belonged to a certain family of magpies. In magpie society, some magpies own territories and others do not. Territory owners consist of small family groups. Usually they have a permanent territory, which means they can defend it, it has good nesting sites, and it has enough resources to feed them all year. They will stay there all their lives.

Then there are magpies who do not own a territory: adults without a partner, young birds who have not established a family, and adults who have been separated from their family. Sometimes these birds form a flock to enhance their survival.

Once Gisela had identified several family groups with a permanent territory, she began to watch each group. To keep track, she gave each magpie a name that matched the white patch of wing feathers on their right side: every bird has a slightly different mark there. If it were the shape of a kidney, that bird would be called Kidney. Or maybe the white feathers looked like a half moon, or a dragon's tail, or a witches hat.

Watching, waiting, recording. Gisela did this for hours every day, several days a week, and loved these glimpses into the natural world. She was noting behaviour that she, and possibly no one else, had seen before. Fieldwork needed precision and commitment, but it was worth it. Every one of her discoveries took her breath away.

She started with vocal development, recording every sound youngsters made from the time they hatched to the time they fledged*, and then during the months they stayed with their parents before being told to leave just before the next breeding season.

Her theory was that magpies are not born with a 'playlist' but continue to learn new songs even as adults. It was always thought that humans were the only animals that continue to learn new things well into adulthood. From her observations, Gisela thought that some birds did the same and now she had to prove it.

She attached a microphone to the base of a nest in one of her observation sites, taping the wire carefully down the tree. Another 30 metres away, she sat with the tape recorder and collected all the sounds they made in the nest, both before feeding and after the parents had left to search for more food. She noted the dates and times.

Back at the university, she transferred the sounds to computers. Many of them were made into sonograms, where sound is turned into visible lines on paper. This showed Gisela all the information about the noise. When she analysed the data of the nestlings and juvenile magpies, she was amazed.

Magpie nestlings start practising their own song from about the second week of life.

They stop practising as soon as a parent bird arrives at the nest.

By the time they fledge, they have their own personal range of songs.

They have a babbling stage, just like human babies, which develops into complex sound.

Magpie youngsters are punished by their parents for using certain sounds like territorial or alarm calls.

Their ability to mimic other species develops before they leave the parent territory.

This brought her back to that very first discovery with Billie. Gisela had wondered back then why Billie had learnt some of Lesley's words instead of Gisela's, and why she hadn't said the words in front of Gisela but only when she was recorded from a distance. Gisela's research showed that this was because magpies never copy their parents' song, and stop practising when the parent comes to the nest; Gisela was Billie's primary carer.

By the time Gisela had finished her PhD on magpies in 2005, she'd spent thousands of hours observing them. She had ten research sites in the Northern Tablelands, with a total of 36 magpies, plus a further 110 birds in 32 family groups between the Northern Tablelands and Coffs Harbour.

She had also shown that magpies keep learning all through their lives, like humans do. Why?

Because learning enhances survival. Learning makes individuals more capable of adapting to new environments, sounds and food availability.

> As well as specific calls such as alarm calls or food calls, magpies also 'improvise', inventing new calls or mimicking sounds.

Gisela had a favourite example. Young magpies without their own territory will move around trying to find a partner and a place that they can call their own. To 'move in', they understand the importance of getting on with the magpies who live nearby: their neighbours. So, they learn how to speak the neighbours' language. Gisela's findings confirmed other studies, showing that when they are settling in, their songs overlap with their neighbours by 25%. They tune in and mimic them in order to get along, to fit in – just like Gisela did, watching *Marine Boy* every day so she could speak to her Australian neighbours.

*

Continuing her work on magpies now that she had finished her PhD, Gisela drove to a new research site, the territory of a family of five magpies. She felt a familiar rush of anticipation. Every site was a chance to record behaviour that would strengthen her evidence to the scientific world and beyond. It was the fuel for her study. But there was something else that excited her: the unknown. Every time she went out to do fieldwork, she had to expect the unexpected. It was like being a detective.

Gisela decided to build an observation hide. This would give her some shelter from the hot sun during a long-term observation. It would also allow her to record the birds' activities and sounds without them knowing. Would this change their behaviour? After all, when humans know they are being watched, they can be self-conscious – in other words, affected by how they think others see them.

Remembering her skills from after-school woodwork classes in Berlin, Gisela constructed a simple wooden frame. She stapled mesh and corrugated sheets to the frame in soft greens and greys to blend in with the bush. There was a small entrance and a wide viewing slit.

As she finished building, a magpie flew to the ground and walked gingerly to the entrance of the hide.

Gisela stepped back to give the bird room to explore. It did just that, eyeing the walls and the space inside. Then it flew to the viewing slit and rested there on the rim. Gisela watched as the bird's head made small, swift jerks, sizing up the new structure that had appeared in its territory.

Suddenly, the magpie spread its wings, lowered its head and raised its feathers. Gisela knew this stance meant it was angry. Next it made a loud alarm call that brought the other magpies to the hide within seconds. Ignoring Gisela standing by, as a team they worked to destroy the hide piece by piece: ripping away the mesh, pulling apart the corrugated sections and demolishing the frame.

Their job done, all five birds flew away.

In her shock, Gisela's main thought was, *how interesting*! She knew already that juvenile magpies play hide-and-seek. She knew also that it was not the colours of the hide that had upset them. It was the moment when the magpie seemed to have understood what the hide would be used for: that Gisela, who'd observed them for weeks, would be able to spy on them unseen. And perhaps *that* was unacceptable to this magpie family.

But this was just a hunch. Meanwhile, Gisela continued to observe the family with no problems. They never swooped her. They even allowed her to come close to their nest.

*

Years later, on a different research site, Gisela had another surprise.

By now she knew many of the magpie calls and she could tell one magpie from another by song alone. She heard an alarm call and looked in the direction of the sound. There she saw a magpie that appeared to be pointing its head forward as it called out. But could it really be pointing? Scientifically, this was something that only humans and some primates had been shown to be able to do.

Then Gisela saw what the magpie was pointing at using its head and beak. Under a bush, half hidden, was a bird of prey. By using an alarm call and showing the others where the danger was by pointing at it with its whole body, the magpie had saved her family.

Pointing involves a thinking process that scientists didn't think birds were capable of. The act of pointing means they are thinking of others (empathy) and want them to see and understand something that could be important to *them*. Those watching the pointing have to understand this message.

It was not enough to see this once. Gisela needed to prove that this was true for other magpies, and in different situations and areas. To do this, she got realistic models of local birds of prey, such as wedge-tailed eagles, and put them in different positions, out in the open or half-hidden in bushes. In other words, she copied the natural environment for her experiment.

In the end, Gisela wrote the first-ever scientific paper about pointing behaviour in birds – in this case, Australian magpies. She proved that humans and primates are not the only species that have this ability. It was yet another breakthrough in understanding bird brains.

*

As Gisela's scientific studies continued, her many observations gave Australia ground-breaking knowledge about magpies. Here is a glimpse of the results of Gisela's studies…

Young magpies learn everything they need to know while being protected by their parents. This takes months and allows their brains to mature.

Young magpies can master the same kinds of games that a 5-year-old human child would understand (like hide-and-seek).

Magpies are complicated! No two magpies behave exactly the same.

There are 8 different alarm calls and many more song types.

Magpies may work together as a team when there is danger.

Magpies may work together to save the life of another type of bird if it is attacked by a bird of prey.

Sometimes a magpie's call means 'Get out of my territory!' but other times it's just for fun – like a human whistle.

Many magpies pair for life. But some magpies get divorced.

Gisela became a Professor – again! – after she wrote her book *Australian Magpie: Biology and Behaviour of an Unusual Songbird*. It became a bestseller. She wrote the book not just for scientists but so that the public could be part of the growing knowledge about Australian songbirds.

13

Bird brain

After a day of giving lectures on bird behaviour and brain function at the university, Gisela was training the dogs. Tipsy was now a mother and there were three puppies to educate: Jenny, Luke and Julie. With so many birds to care for – injured, confused, and certainly frightened when they first arrived – it was important to have well-behaved domestic dogs.

Lesley and Gisela had plans to write a book together about wild dogs like dingoes, jackals, wolves – and of course, foxes, the very first creature to captivate Gisela as a child at the Berlin Zoo.

Afterwards, Gisela left the dogs to play-wrestle on the lawn and went to the intensive-care aviary to check on Philip.

Philip was a galah who had been brought to Gisela by the local vet after he'd treated the poor bird's two broken wings. All the vet knew was that Philip was 75 years old, had been a pet bird all his life and was kept by more than one owner. The galah was very ill but the vet knew that Gisela was not one to give up.

Galahs get layers of knobbly skin around their eyes as they age. It's a bit like counting the ring marks of a tree. With other birds, age may be difficult to tell. Sulphur-crested cockatoos, for instance, can be 50 years old and look the same as they did as teenagers.

A few months after he had arrived, Philip looked much healthier and most of his feathers had grown back. Although he couldn't fly, he was quite active.

One afternoon, Philip did something amazing. He had learned all the dog names.

'Tipsy! Jenny! Luke! Julie!'

The dogs bounded over to the galah. Once they were in front of him, Philip said quite clearly, 'Sit!'

Three of the dogs obeyed him but one just stared. When the galah glared and hissed at the disobedient puppy, he quickly did as he was told. Gisela carried on observing from a distance. Finally, when the dogs were sitting patiently and seemed to be awaiting the next instruction, Philip casually walked away from them. The dogs had no idea what to do next! Gisela saw a swagger and heard a cackle of mischief from Philip. The sound he was making might even have been something like a giggle.

Philip is not only highly intelligent, it seems as if he has a sense of humour, she thought. This was something highly disputed amongst scientists.

Although her rescue work was separate from her scientific work, it sparked ideas for further study. She was curious to find out just how brainy the galah was as a species. She was also intrigued about the brainpower of sulphur-crested cockatoos.

In the dictionary, the word 'birdbrained' is defined as 'a stupid person'. Gisela had seen how false that was, and through her research she had joined the scientists who were showing that to the rest of the world.

*

The rehabilitation work never stopped. Sometimes the vet brought Gisela a bird and sometimes it was the other way round. Today she presented him with an injured wedge-tailed eagle.

'Couldn't you have brought me an easier bird?' he said as the eagle struggled in Gisela's arms, despite having multiple fractures.

'I thought you'd like a challenge,' Gisela replied with a chuckle. 'These are magnificent birds. We've got to do whatever we can to fix it. Birds of prey are so necessary for healthy ecosystems.'

The scientific name for a **wedge-tailed eagle** is *Aquila audax*, which means 'bold eagle'. They can soar as high as 2 km and can be spotted by the distinctive diamond-shape of their tail feathers.

The wedge-tailed eagle is Australia's largest bird of prey with a wingspan of two and a half metres. Although not as swift as other birds of prey, wedge-tailed eagles are skilled hunters who choose from a wide menu. They can swoop on a running rabbit or wallaby and kill it instantly with powerful talons. They also eat possums, foxes, kangaroo joeys, gliders, large reptiles, and some birds. They are so strong that they can fly off with an animal heavier than their own body weight.

'We'll have to X-ray it,' said the vet, 'but I can only do that if the bird is completely still. I'll need to give it an anaesthetic.'

'Aren't there risks with that in birds?'

'There are. I'll need to be as accurate as possible when I calculate the dose. It's easy to get it wrong.'

'But I don't think we've got a choice,' Gisela said. 'If this bird can't fly, it can't survive in the wild.'

Later that night, the eagle was in one of Gisela's intensive-care aviaries. The good news was that the vet thought the fractures could be fixed. The bad news was that the bird had not woken up from the anaesthetic. There was a chance it never would.

With the nights getting cold in Armidale, Gisela decided to bring the unconscious eagle inside. Weighing three kilograms, about the same as a newborn baby but a good deal larger, the bird lay completely still in Gisela's arms while she walked around the house, rocking it and trying to make it stir from the deep sleep caused by the anaesthetic.

At three o'clock in the morning, her arms and back ached so much that she had to sit down. She fell asleep instantly on the sofa, the bird resting on her lap.

Two hours later, she woke with a start. Light was seeping into the room and she remembered that she had a wedge-tailed eagle on her lap. His eyes were wide open, his mighty beak a few centimetres away from her face.

'Congratulations, you've made it,' she said. She held her breath, wondering what the bird would do next. He lowered his head and let it rest on her forearm, clearly not intending to harm the person who had comforted him all night. Gisela could see that his eyes were still open. Quietly, they watched the sunrise.

With the fractures fixed, Gisela released the eagle back into the wild some four weeks later. She went on to rescue and heal many more birds of prey after him. One thing she noted was that impressive hunters like goshawks and peregrine falcons rarely showed gratitude for being helped. In fact, sometimes they'd nip her as she released them. Kookaburras were the same, even when she'd raised them from tiny babies. This didn't faze Gisela, because she saw that as a good outcome – wild birds *should* be wild.

It was also true that special moments happened all the time with the birds she'd rehabilitated. There was an Eastern rosella which she named Mini. Gisela had rescued her from underneath the poor frozen body of Mini's mother, who'd tried to shield her babies from a hailstorm. Only Mini was alive.

Gisela raised Mini, who flew freely around the garden when she was at full health. Then one day three wild rosellas started to hang around as if inviting her to join them, which Mini eventually did.

Gisela was so happy that Mini would have friends who could teach her how to be a rosella.

Later, Gisela saw four rosellas in the sky. One of them separated from the others and flew towards her. The bird stopped on her shoulder and nibbled her ear before flying off to catch up with the others. These few seconds were Mini's way of saying a final goodbye.

Despite their bright colours, the plumage of an **Eastern rosella** is patterned so that it creates a good camouflage to help the birds avoid detection by potential predators.

14

Haven

One New Year's Day in Armidale, a huge thunder-cloud was building. The sky rumbled, turning darker, and the rain that had started to fall became hail. Gisela could hear it drumming on the roof. Through the window, the hail ricocheted off the ground in hard balls of ice the size of limes.

Armidale is well-placed for storms. Some have been so severe that they've caused damage to thousands of houses and cars. For Gisela, the worry was that livestock and wildlife could get hurt. Animals become disorientated during the chaos of storms and hailstones can injure or kill them, falling from the sky at 60 kilometres per hour or even faster. All creatures are vulnerable. Grey-headed flying foxes can be knocked out of trees; possums, lorikeets, kookaburras, even kangaroos in wide-open spaces can be killed by giant hailstones.

Finally, the hail turned back into raindrops and carried on lashing trees and bushes for hours. Gisela's rescue birds were safe from harm but what about the thousands of creatures who shared the beautiful Northern Tablelands?

The next day when the professors went out to check the damage, something struck them. It was eerily quiet. They were used to the early morning marketplace chatter of wild birds, and the buzzing of insects like mud wasps and katydids. But there was no sound of life. It was like the aftermath of a bushfire.

From out of nowhere, a flash of grey caught their attention. Two adult tawny frogmouths landed in the garden with a younger, smaller one that must be their offspring.

'I know these tawnies,' said Gisela.

'Are these the two you raised from chicks?' asked Lesley. Gisela was in no doubt.

'And now they've brought us their baby. Looking for some comfort and shelter after what must have been a very stressful day for them.'

The arrival of the tawnies was followed by a return of familiar sounds. More wild birds came out of hiding and started up their song. Gisela was confident that the little family of tawny frogmouths would stay for a while, at least until the young one was ready to go out on its own. She found this species very loveable. As little ones they're like fluffy toys. As adults they are incredible shapeshifters. Their stunning feathers camouflage with the shape and colour of tree bark. She found it so endearing that they would simply sit still and pretend not to be there. It was a very successful survival skill.

> The **Tawny Frogmouth**, scientific name *Podargus strigoides*, is the largest bird that can lower its own body temperature (go into torpor*) to save energy.

Gisela still had her mate, Tawny, who could not survive in the wild on his own because of brain damage. Now she was looking forward to watching these new parents.

Like magpies and many other Australian birds, tawny frogmouths are another example of dedicated parents. When parent tawnies roost with their young, the mother and father squash the babies between them. When it comes to hunting for food, the parents take turns: the father is the day-parent while the mother goes out hunting at dawn; then the roles are reversed. The chicks are never alone.

This family had not been with Gisela long before changes occurred. The young one became a teenager – in bird months, that is. Gisela couldn't believe how much trouble one tawny frogmouth could be. The youngster was totally reckless: flying in a terrifying manner and staying out in the open when it was supposed to be camouflaging or asleep. The parents had no choice but to follow it around, trying to coax it to be more sensible.

One baking hot day, the teenage tawny flew onto the roof of an aviary. Dutifully, the parents followed and tried to coax it back to safety, but the teenage tawny wasn't budging. As if it were not dangerous enough being visible to birds of prey, the roof was made of corrugated iron, which meant it was getting hotter as the afternoon wore on. Gisela got a ladder and some cardboard, which she dampened with cool water. Then she climbed up and slid it under their poor hot feet. At least that would help the parents a little bit – the rest was up to them. Tawny frogmouths are very stoic – they did not even try to fly away when she was carrying out this rescue operation.

After that, she noticed the teenage tawny improving its hunting skills. She spotted it catching a Christmas beetle in flight, which it took to a branch and munched.

She was also watching when the tawny parents decided that it was time for some tough love: they shoved their offspring off the roosting spot to start life alone as an adult. Gisela recorded it so she had evidence of the precise behaviour that meant *leave our territory*. She noted that this seemed abrupt with tawnies; magpie parents and juveniles, on the other hand, take longer to reach the deal about leaving home. The teenage tawny sat in one spot all night making a noise that sounded like the soft crying of a baby. It was a heart-wrenching, whimpering sound. Gisela felt so sorry for it. But she could not interfere with this important part of his life.

The next morning, the teenager had gone. And with that, Gisela was ready to start work on a new book. This time, much of her fieldwork took place in the middle of the night. The Australian bush in darkness was another revelation to her. A moonlit sky peppered with stars and the silhouette of a tawny; it was breathtaking.

After she had collected as much data as she could from wild or rehabilitated frogmouths, and hand-raised many of them, she was ready to produce a meaningful study of every aspect of tawny frogmouth life, from their emotions to their social behaviour and habitats.

*

There were so many hellos and goodbyes on Gisela and Lesley's property, from the biggest bird of prey to the sweetest rosella. But like Philip the Galah, some rejected or mistreated pets became permanent house guests.

> Male and female cockatoos can only be told apart by their eyes. Males have dark brown eyes; females have a reddish tinge to the brown in theirs.

An injured sulphur-crested cockatoo, also a pet, was brought to Gisela. His flying days were over because his flight bones had been broken and left untreated. He had hardly any feathers, barely moved and didn't communicate. It didn't seem to be a happy life but because it looked as if this bird was staying, she gave him a name: Pumpkin.

Over time it became clear that Pumpkin's past life had traumatised him. He just needed love and care. It took years of perseverance, but after five years his feathers had all come back and were a gleaming white.

He started communicating and talking, and eventually he became playful. When he ripped apart Gisela's decking – something cockatoos would usually do on gum trees to sharpen their beaks – Gisela sprayed him with the garden hose to put him off. Pumpkin merely stretched out his wings and welcomed the shower. And then carried on chewing up the deck.

By now Gisela was one of the world's experts in the behaviour of Australian birds. What the world was learning, thanks in part to her work, was that some Australian birds have the same problem-solving abilities as chimpanzees, despite the size differences in their brains. Sulphur-crested cockatoos like Pumpkin, or galahs like Philip, are among these. So are other Psittacines (parrots and cockatoos) and the Corvids (ravens, magpies, crows).

It wasn't just important to study the intelligence (cognition) of birds but also how they *feel*. In the past, people had assumed that birds didn't experience emotion apart from aggression or fear. Now Gisela had discovered that this was wrong. She had observed every feeling from affection to jealousy, joy to grief, selfishness to generosity.

She had seen tawny frogmouths grieve for a lost partner, or cry when it was time to leave home. She'd seen a magpie cheat on his partner, with a look over his shoulder as if he knew he was doing the wrong thing. Her studies of magpies proved that they remember the faces of humans they find threatening. And a noisy miner that Gisela had hand-raised saved one of her puppies from a lace monitor by swooping the giant lizard and raising the alarm.

Gisela was not working to make birds more 'human' but to understand what a bird's abilities truly are. Birds have complicated lives, brains, and feelings, too.

And if you ever go to Gisela's house, there is one golden rule: say hello to Pumpkin first.

15

Mission

August, 2020.

Today is Gisela's birthday. In recent years she has recovered from some serious illnesses. A few weeks ago, she had another operation, finally paying the price for the malnutrition of her childhood. The recovery is painful and difficult. It is frustrating not to be able to walk around her property or drive her car, and she cannot take in injured birds or do fieldwork at the moment. But that will pass.

She casts her mind back over the years of her work with birds.

*

Despite this work starting later in her life, she has become regarded worldwide as an eminent ornithologist.

As she's travelled the world, connecting with other scientists who specialise in animal behaviour, she has noticed that the study of bird behaviour isn't given priority everywhere. There is always politics involved in science which is shown in the decisions to give money to some areas of study and not others.

Gisela believes that Australia should put more funding into the study of animal behaviour because of the climate emergency affecting many vulnerable species. For instance, magpies stop feeding when the temperature is higher than 27 degrees, so global warming will impact on their populations severely. This is true of many other native birds.

One of Gisela's early trips included a visit to Berlin and reunion in Munich with her 'little brother'. It was wonderful to see him again, and to revisit the place where she had grown up. But returning to Germany didn't feel like going home. Australia has become home. There is no other place Gisela would rather be than the land where the modern songbirds and parrots evolved, dating back millions of years, making these species among the most important in the world for her in scientific study.

*

After a lifetime of long journeys and big changes, Gisela made one more move. She and Lesley relocated their work, home and bird haven to the coast of northern New South Wales. Much of Gisela's fieldwork had already taken place in that area, which is rich in wildlife. There are nearly 400 species of birds. Fourteen of those are globally threatened. Gisela bought a patch of sub-tropical rainforest nearby, on which she built a cottage herself.

Gisela and Lesley worked together on another book called *Birds: Their Habits and Skills*. After that, Gisela wrote an award-winning children's book called *Famous Australian Birds*, which she dedicated to her three much-loved grandchildren and her two nephews and niece.

As Gisela's mission has expanded, her time has become split many ways: ground-breaking research into how birds think and behave, writing books, rehabilitating injured birds, writing for scientific journals, magazines and newspapers, consulting on international TV documentaries, answering listener calls on radio shows, giving lectures, speaking at literary festivals and international conferences, recording podcasts, replying to emails from the public about her books or sick birds they've found, training wildlife carers, talking to journalists, helping animal welfare and environmental groups to protect birds and their habitats, and one more activity that she considers very important: talking in schools.

When Gisela has visited schools, with formal permission, Tawny has gone with her. He'd sit on her hand and for ten minutes the students could watch him or gently stroke his feathers if they liked. For many, it was the first time they'd ever seen a tawny frogmouth. For some, it created a spark. The spark might not show up straight away but bury itself and wait for the right moment. This was how it had happened for Gisela and her dusty little fox chained up in Berlin Zoo.

She's had one goal: to spread knowledge. Gisela's hope is that if more people understand their native birds and how extraordinary they are, they will strive to protect them.

Gisela's work with the largest wildlife rescue organisation in Australia goes back 27 years. One day they asked her to help a kookaburra. It had been found by a little boy, aged eight, who was able to point out exactly where he'd found it.

Gisela treated the bird until it was healthy enough to be released. Then she called the boy's mum and asked if they'd like to come and watch the release near the roosting tree. The hope was that the young kookaburra's family would let the bird come back to them. In the end, it wasn't just the boy and his mum but also his dad and two siblings who came to see what they hoped would be a happy reunion.

Gisela explained, 'Once it reaches the roosting tree, it should shake itself. This means it recognises this spot. Then the other kookaburras should come and sit next to it. And then comes the final step, just you wait.'

The boy and his family were transfixed, crouching low and staying quiet.

Step-by-step, everything that Gisela had described happened before their eyes. The final step arrived: one bird started with a low, gulping chuckle.

The chuckle built to a full belly laugh and all the other kookaburras joined in. The air was filled with an incredible sound – *koo-koo-koo-koo-kaa-kaa-kaa!* – which meant that the bird was welcomed back home.

> The kookaburra is the biggest member of the Kingfisher family. They can live for more than 20 years and have the same partner for life.

Years down the line, Gisela received a phone call out of the blue from the boy's mum. She wanted Gisela to know that because of that day, her son was studying to be a vet. The injured kookaburra had been his spark.

*

Gisela has received several awards for services to wildlife. She was added to a list of the top 100 ornithologists in the world. She was made a fellow of the International Ornithological Union, an elected fellow of the Royal Society of NSW, became patron of the Dingo Conservation Society, the Bird Advocacy Foundation, a life member of the International Primatological Society, a member of the Centre for Veterinary Education, the Australian Psychological Society, Honorary Professor at the Queensland Brain Institute, and so on, and so on, and so on!

As well as being the author of over 250 articles, Gisela has so far written 23 books, eight of those co-authored with Lesley Rogers. Gisela and Lesley were the first two women declared Emeritus Professor in their university, a title given for life to honour distinguished work. Gisela was awarded a rare honorary Doctor of Science degree for her contribution to scholarship by the University of New England. And Lesley was the only female academic at that university at the time to be elected fellow to the Australian Academy of Science.

Gisela's book *Bird Minds* (2015) brought together all her research of native Australian songbirds and parrots on the subject of learning, memory and innovation. Her book *Bird Bonds* (2019) showed how humans and birds are more alike than we thought when it comes to helping friends, choosing partners and sticking to family. Her books on Australian magpies and tawny frogmouths were so popular and enduring that updated editions have been published to keep up with new research.

Each time Gisela finishes a book, people say: 'You know so much about birds!' And Gisela thinks: *but there is so much more to discover.*

*

August, 2020.

'I'm driving us to Boambee for your birthday,' says Lesley.

It's Gisela's favourite look out. She might be recovering from a major operation but she is tired of these four walls and determined not to let anything hold her back.

The view from Boambee Headland is out of this world. From here you can see whales during their migration season. White-bellied sea eagles soar overhead.

There is a birthday cake. And then suddenly, there is a second birthday cake! A group of friends surprise her by meeting her at the lookout, with mountains of food to feast on and parcels to unwrap.

In the winter sunshine, Gisela feels her mind transported. As she breathes the salt air and watches the ocean sparkle, it stirs a memory from long ago,

a time when she was feeling intense pain while looking at something very beautiful. Gisela the small, bullied child with a stutter. The Grunewald forest. Her beautiful Nan.

This is how she has survived. Clinging to kindness, noticing beauty and seeking wisdom. She learnt this from her grandmother.

'There's a new research article I'm going to write,' she tells her friends. 'It's about the importance of play behaviour in birds for growing a large brain and living a long life.'

'It's very difficult to get published in the science journal that you want to send it to,' Lesley warns. 'Not that you're going to let that scare you off.'

'You know me, I'll recover from this operation and then it's full steam ahead with my work,' Gisela says. 'We need to know exactly how we can help birds survive in a world that is ever more difficult for them.'

In 2020, Gisela made an important discovery: birds that engaged in play behaviour with each other had larger brains than those that didn't or who played only by themselves.

'And *all* our wildlife,' Lesley adds.

They are all quiet for a moment. The ocean sounds like whispering. Gisela breathes the salt air and smiles, thinking of her future work with birds: cracking more codes and debunking more myths. She has hope, she has determination, and for Professor Gisela Kaplan there is much more work to be done.

Glossary

▷ **Anti-Semitism:** anti-Jewish hatred.

▷ **Budgerigar:** a small parrot that evolved in Australia at least 4 million years ago, according to fossil evidence. The scientific name is *Melopsittacus undulatus*. Budgies were bred as pet birds from the 1850s and became the most favoured pet bird all over the world.

▷ **Cosmology**: the study of how the universe came to exist, what its structure is like, and what the future of the universe may be.

▷ **Nazi concentration camps:** From 1933 to 1945, Nazi Germany and its allies established more than 44,000 camps for a range of purposes, including forced labour, detention of people thought to be 'enemies of the state', and dedicated ones for mass murder – which is where many Jewish Europeans were killed.

▷ **Evolution:** the way that living things adapt and change over many years.

▷ **Fledged:** when a bird has acquired the feathers necessary for flight and has left the nest.

▷ **Mobile libraries:** before the Internet, these gave people free access to information and literature. The first one was a horse-drawn wagon (Britain, 1857). There are still mobile libraries in parts of Australia.

- **Nestling:** a bird that is too young to leave the nest.

- **Night school:** some high schools in Australia used to offer classes in the evening to adults who hadn't completed high school, or to migrants whose qualifications weren't recognised in Australia.

- **Opera:** a theatrical performance consisting of a story that has been set to music, and staged with scenery, costumes and movement.

- **Ornithologists:** people who study the branch of science devoted to birds.

- **Rabies:** a deadly virus that is usually spread to humans through an animal bite. Australia is rabies-free.

- **Wildlife rehabilitation:** treating and caring for injured, sick, or orphaned native animals and returning them to their families and territories as soon as possible after they have recovered.

- **Rhodesian Ridgebacks:** partly derived from African wild dogs and bred to be hunters, they are large, muscular and intelligent as well as affectionate and loyal. With wheaten or brown short hair, they have a standout ridge of hair along their backs.

- **Torpor:** a state of lowered activity (including reduced heart rate and body temperature) to preserve energy in harmful environmental conditions.

- **Vocalisation:** the process of making sounds with the voice.

About Emily Gale

Emily Gale grew up in London, where the most common backyard birds are pigeons, robins, magpies, blackbirds and sparrows. As a child she was more of a dog-person, sharing her bed most nights with a fiercely protective dachshund named Ted.

In 2008 Emily migrated to Australia, where she continued to be a dog-person (Charlie, a labradoodle), gradually became a cat-person (Harry, a tabby, and Tinsel, a tortoiseshell) and more recently became fascinated by Australian birdlife. She lives near a part of the Yarra river in Melbourne where well over 100 different species of birds have been identified. (She regrets to say that she has not yet seen them all, but is working on it.)

Emily writes for children and teenagers. Her junior fiction character, *Eliza Boom*, is about a young inventor and has been translated into many different languages. Her YA novels have been shortlisted for several awards, including her latest one *I Am Out With Lanterns*.

Lightning Source UK Ltd.
Milton Keynes UK
UKHW012000120921
390455UK00002B/481